Scottish Highlands New Year Ball

De-ann Black

Paperback edition published 2024

Scottish Highlands New Year Ball

ISBN: 9798300906245

Scottish Highlands New Year Ball is the seventh book in the Scottish Loch Romance series.

Romance:
Scottish Highlands New Year Ball
Ballroom Dancing Christmas Romance
Christmas Ballroom Dancing
Autumn Romance
Knitting & Starlight
Knitting Bee
The Sweetest Waltz
Sweet Music
Love & Lyrics
Christmas Weddings
Fairytale Christmas on the Island
The Cure for Love at Christmas
Vintage Dress Shop on the Island
Scottish Island Fairytale Castle
Scottish Loch Summer Romance
Scottish Island Knitting Bee
Sewing & Mending Cottage
Knitting Shop by the Sea
Colouring Book Cottage
Knitting Cottage
Oops! I'm the Paparazzi, Again
The Bitch-Proof Wedding
Embroidery Cottage
The Dressmaker's Cottage
The Sewing Shop
Heather Park
The Tea Shop by the Sea
The Bookshop by the Seaside
The Sewing Bee

The Quilting Bee
Snow Bells Wedding
Snow Bells Christmas
Summer Sewing Bee
The Chocolatier's Cottage
Christmas Cake Chateau
The Beemaster's Cottage
The Sewing Bee By The Sea
The Flower Hunter's Cottage
The Christmas Knitting Bee
The Sewing Bee & Afternoon Tea
Shed In The City
The Bakery By The Seaside
The Christmas Chocolatier
The Christmas Tea Shop & Bakery
The Bitch-Proof Suit

Action/Thrillers:

Knight in Miami.
Agency Agenda.
Love Him Forever.
Someone Worse.

Electric Shadows.
The Strife of Riley.
Shadows of Murder.

Colouring books:

Summer Nature. Flower Nature. Summer Garden. Spring Garden. Autumn Garden. Sea Dream. Festive Christmas. Christmas Garden. Flower Bee. Wild Garden. Flower Hunter. Stargazer Space. Christmas Theme. Faerie Garden Spring. Scottish Garden Seasons. Bee Garden.

Embroidery books:

Floral Garden Embroidery Patterns
Floral Spring Embroidery Patterns
Christmas & Winter Embroidery Patterns
Floral Nature Embroidery Designs
Scottish Garden Embroidery Designs

Contents

CHAPTER ONE

Music and dance
My heart is in tune with you
Rhythm and romance
I promise my love is true...

Laurie breathed in the cold, fresh air, stepping out of his luxury cabin within the estate of the magnificent Scottish castle set in the Scottish Highlands. Everything sparkled in the dazzling morning light under a blanket of snow.

Situated near a beautiful loch and the village's main street with its pretty shops, the castle had a view of the spectacular winter scenery. It had snowed again the previous night, ensuring a winter's fairytale effect of snow throughout the estate and surrounding forest.

It was the last week of December, just after Christmas and Boxing Day, and he'd been up before the dawn, trying to finish the song he'd been writing for his latest album. A famous and successful singer and musician, in his early thirties, Laurie had played his keyboard and guitar in his cabin attempting to create the right lyrics for the song.

Laurie was currently staying in one of the cabins on the castle's estate while a local house he'd recently purchased was being refurbished to include a private music recording studio.

As the morning sunlight glinted over the tops of the frosted trees, he decided to go for a run to clear his thoughts — and find the romantic lyrics for his next hit. He could hear the music, the melody, but the words were elusive.

Dressed to tackle the terrain in training gear, dark blue joggers with a sky blue top that suited his tall, lean, broad–shouldered build, Laurie started to run, hearing his boots crunch through the snow.

The love I feel for you

You know my heart is true...

Laurie sighed deeply and ran on, forging a path through the long grass, his gorgeous pale grey eyes blinking against the bright winter sunlight that highlighted the trees against the cold blue sky.

He dipped below the frozen overhanging branches of an archway of trees, dripping with diamonds of ice.

Emerging from the trees, the forest opened out into a vast snowscape.

As he broke into a rhythmic jog, he heard the beat of the music. Come on, he urged himself, sweeping a frustrated hand through his light brown hair, pushing it back from his handsome face. Find the words to tell Sylvia how much you love her, and will always love her. Lyrics written from the heart would surely bring their own success.

Sylvia filled one of the sweetie jars with chocolate toffees and put it in the front window of the sweet shop.

She peered out at the quaint shops lining the village main street, all adorned with festive decorations.

'The street looks lovely covered with snow,' Sylvia said to Muira, her aunt. They owned the shop,

2

and wore pretty pink aprons with a multi–coloured sweet print.

The sweet shop had been closed on Christmas Day and Boxing Day, and now they were catching up with the busy online orders, and selling everything from their Scottish tablet to Sylvia's chocolate robins as local customers were eager to stock up on sweets for the New Year celebrations.

Hogmanay, the last day of the year, was celebrated in style, and the shop's champagne and whisky truffles were popular. With only a few days until Hogmanay, there was a sense of excitement in the village.

Muira was busy bagging the online orders and glanced out the window at the snowy morning. 'We'll need to wrap up warm tonight for the crafting bee up at the castle.'

It was the first crafting bee night after Christmas, and the last one before the New Year ball.

'Yes, it'll be cosy at the castle, but a freezing cold night to head up there.' Sylvia came over to the counter and started to help pack the orders ready to take them to the post office later. An attractive young woman in her early thirties, she had shoulder–length blonde hair tied back in a ponytail, and had moved to the village to work with Muira. Sylvia had previously worked for a bakery in Edinburgh and trained in confectionery making.

Since the summer, Sylvia had been dating Laurie when he'd arrived at the castle to take a creative break in one of the cabins.

'I'm taking my needle felting with me.' Sylvia had learned needle felting from Muira, and enjoyed quilting too.

Muira, in her fifties, was a keen knitter and crafter, and was dating Sean, a local beemaster.

Romance had been in the air locally for a few seasons, with several new couples finding love. One couple recently became engaged in the autumn, and another couple got married just before Christmas.

'I'll take my knitting,' said Muira. 'I'm starting a new cardigan in a lovely soft double knit yarn.'

'That'll be nice,' Sylvia agreed.

'What about your dress for the New Year ball?'

Sylvia smiled excitedly. 'Penny says she's bringing it to the bee tonight. She's finished the alterations. And added a few sequins to the straps.'

'Oh, it sounds lovely,' said Muira.

Penny was an expert at sewing and mending and loved making dresses from the past like new again. She ran her pre–loved vintage fashion business from her cottage by the loch. She'd recently been a snow bride when she married Neil, the local goldsmith.

'It's a gorgeous vintage evening dress,' Sylvia revealed. 'Penny has altered it to fit perfectly.' It was pale yellow layers of silk and chiffon, and had a fairytale quality that suited Sylvia's slim build and delicate features.

Sylvia was attending the ball, as were other members of the crafting bee. Penny sold bargain dresses, and several of the bee members intended wearing one of the evening dresses they'd bought from her. The dresses were all hand–picked, pre–loved to be loved once more.

But Sylvia had a talent for playing the piano, and the laird had invited her to play the baby grand piano in the castle's piano bar as part of the New Year festivities. She'd played at Christmastime, and Laurie had performed too, playing his guitar. Now they were scheduled to perform again at the New Year ball. So she felt her dress had to be extra special for the performance.

Sylvia had loved the dress with its ballgown quality the moment she saw it advertised on Penny's website.

Sylvia's dress had previously been worn for a stage performance in a theatre in Edinburgh, the nearest city to the village. A few local residents travelled to Edinburgh regularly on business, including the castle's laird.

Gaven, the laird, owner of the castle, pinned a note up beside a poster in the castle's stylish reception.

The castle's decor was a mix of classic and modern, with plush tartan carpeting, lamps and chandeliers, bright and inviting. The front entrance door was open and the morning's glow from the snow outside poured in.

The poster advertised the forthcoming New Year ball. It was less than a week away. The recent Christmas ball had been a success with local village residents and guests from the castle's hotel facilities. Everyone was now looking forward to the exciting New Year ball. A lavish buffet was planned by the castle's head chef. Musical entertainment included a performance by Laurie in the large function room, playing his guitar and singing a few of his popular songs while couples danced on the spacious dance floor. Sylvia was listed to play the baby grand piano in the castle's piano bar. And a piper was scheduled to play the bagpipes outside the castle on the approach of midnight to ring in the New Year.

Gaven's note stated that the dancing ranged from traditional ballroom waltzing to ceilidh dances.

In his early thirties, Gaven was tall and kept himself fit by running around the loch, often in the evenings, and in the estate whatever the weather. His rich, auburn hair was stylishly–cut and suited his classic features. He was always well–dressed in tailored suits or kilted. This morning, he wore a suit, and his grey–green eyes viewed the details on the poster that advised those attending the ball to wear kilts or evening attire to suit the celebratory ball.

Jessy and Walter worked behind the reception desk. They were two key members of staff. The laird relied on them to help with the efficient running of the castle's hotel facilities including the luxury cabins set in niches around the estate.

Jessy was in her fifties and wore her hair in a tidy chignon. A keen crafter, she intended taking her knitting along to the crafting bee night.

Walter, a mature man with a cheerful nature, helped deal with guests at the reception, and worked as the castle's handyman.

'Guests and others attending the New Year ball have been wondering what dances are included,'

Gaven said to Jessy and Walter. 'So I've written a note to explain that instead of our usual ceilidh dancing I'm adding ballroom dances too.'

'I think that sounds great,' Jessy enthused. 'The winter and Christmas balls were wonderful, especially as many of us had learned to improve our waltzing from lessons with Ian.'

'I enjoyed the waltzing at Christmas,' said Walter. 'Adding a bit of ballroom to the ceilidh dancing is an excellent idea.'

'I've included information on the formal dress code,' said Gaven. 'Evening dresses for the ladies, full–length.'

'Worn with pumps or shoes suitable for dancing the night away,' Jessy chimed–in.

Gaven nodded. 'Explain the details to the guests, though most of them know this is a dress to impress ball. Traditional Highland evening attire. Kilts or evening suits worn with a tartan waistcoat, tie or waistband. Though I expect most men will be kilted.'

'I'm wearing my kilt,' said Walter.

Jessy read the note. 'I notice you've said that there are reels, jigs and waltzes, but foxtrots and other ballroom dances are encouraged too.'

'Yes,' Gaven said firmly. 'A mix of dances to celebrate the New Year.'

'Folk should manage to waltz, but what about the other ballroom dances like the foxtrot?' said Jessy. 'Will Ian be giving any lessons beforehand?'

Ian was a professional dancer for stage and other performances and contests. He'd recently moved from Edinburgh to live in the village and was dating another new resident, Rose, an expert quilter. Their romance was new but going well, and they'd enjoyed Christmas together.

'I'm going to discuss this with Ian,' Gaven explained. 'I've invited him up for breakfast and a chat about teaching ballroom dancing one afternoon in the castle's function room.'

Jessy's face lit up with excitement. 'I hope he says yes. I'd love to learn more dances from Ian.'

'Count me in as well,' said Walter.

'I'll do my best to persuade him,' Gaven promised.

Rose walked across the snowy field towards Ian's cottage.

The only other property in the field was Rose's cottage. Ian owned the larger of the two cottages on the far side of the field. She'd recently moved from the city to live in the small, rented cottage and loved the vintage styling and homely atmosphere. She'd moved in before the snowfall when the field looked beautifully untamed with its long grass and wild flowers.

The snow created the illusion of it being well–kept. One of the beemasters' fields edged it on one side. Come the spring, when the snow melted, the wildness would be on show again. On this side of the loch it was mainly wild fields leading into the heart of the countryside.

Rose had promised herself she'd tend the garden around her cottage when the milder weather allowed. As had Ian, though the fire pit he'd added to his garden was currently well–used on cold, snowy nights.

Wrapped up in her cream wool coat, pink knitted hat and scarf, she'd been down to the main street to buy fresh bread and scones from Bradoch's bakery and picked up a fresh loaf for Ian while she was there.

It was barely a two minute walk from the main street to the cottages dotted around the loch, and only another couple of minutes from the loch up to the field where her cottage was situated across from Ian. From being new neighbours, they'd become a new couple and were planning a future together.

Rose was slender, thirty, and had shoulder–length dark chestnut hair, blue eyes and a lovely pale complexion. Although a quilter, she could knit, and wore a jumper she'd knitted herself. She sold quilts and quilted items from her website along with her popular patterns.

Trudging through the deep snow, while enjoying being out in the brisk air, Rose walked up to Ian's front door and knocked. She could hear lively music filtering out from his living room where he had a makeshift dance floor that he used to keep himself in shape and practise his dancing. The extension added plenty of space to the large living room for a dance floor.

Rose opened the door and walked in. 'Ian! It's me,' she called to him above the upbeat song.

Ian was in full flow, doing what she'd recently learned were voltas in a samba. The samba consisted of a lively bouncing motion with a lot of hip action. Ian didn't do casual, even early in the morning. He wore a white shirt, black trousers and highly polished dance shoes.

'Ian!' Rose repeated.

From his reaction as he glanced at her, she'd clearly startled him, but equally, his smile showed how pleased he was to see her. He bounded over.

Wrapping her in his arms, he lifted her up in a welcoming hug and kissed the breath from her. She ended up more breathless than him without dancing a step.

'I brought you a fresh loaf from the bakery.' She held up her grocery bag.

'Thank you. I haven't had breakfast yet.' He put her bag aside and pulled her into close hold. 'Gaven has invited me to have breakfast with him at the castle.'

Rose gazed up at him. Ian was tall, with a lean–muscled build, clean–shaven with well–styled dark hair and turquoise blue eyes that were the bluest she'd ever seen. 'That probably means he wants you to teach ballroom dance lessons again.'

Ian nodded. 'It does. Gaven wants to chat about holding an afternoon ballroom dance lesson in the castle's function room before the New Year ball.'

'That's not long now,' Rose remarked.

'I know, but I've agreed to have breakfast and a chat.' Ian checked the time. 'I'll need to get going soon. But do you want to take a spin around the floor with me? Try out your foxtrot?'

'I'm finding the foxtrot as tricky as you said it would be,' she admitted.

'Then you should practise any chance you get. Put your shoes on.'

Rose took her coat, hat and scarf off and changed out of her boots into the ballroom dance shoes Ian had bought for her as a gift. She kept her ballroom shoes tucked under his Christmas tree.

'Remember your posture,' Ian reminded her as he began to foxtrot with her.

Rose righted her posture and danced with Ian until it was time for him to head up to the castle.

Ian drove her the short distance across the field to her cottage and dropped her off.

Rose waved to him from her front door and then went inside to make tea and toast for breakfast. She planned a morning of quilting in her cottage, snuggled up in a sewing snow day.

Ian's car navigated the narrow path leading down to the loch. The water was smooth as glass. Despite the cold, he opened the window as he drove along.

The loch and countryside merged beautifully, and the sea was only a ten minute drive away. Some mornings, he could pick up the scent of the sea along with the fresh country air.

Breathing deeply, he headed on, and took the forest road that led up to the castle. Tall trees lined the forest road, some arching over and iced white with snow.

Moving from Edinburgh to the village had made him realise that he was starting a new and exciting phase of his dancing career. Teaching wasn't part of his plans, but he was happy to help the laird during the festive party season. He'd already taught a handful of dance lessons in afternoons leading up to Christmas. Another afternoon lesson wouldn't crowd his schedule as he'd yet to start rehearsals for a dance show in the new year.

Ian had accepted the role he'd played before in a show that was a success in a theatre in Edinburgh the previous new year. The director wanted him to do another six–week run of it, and rehearsals started in late January.

He planned to drive back and forth to Edinburgh for most of the performances, ensuring his new romance with Rose would flourish as he continued his ballroom dancing success. And Rose would build her quilting business from her cottage.

Rose had no aspirations to be a professional dancer, but Ian had been teaching her one of his favourite dances, the foxtrot, in time for the New Year ball at the castle.

Ian planned to wear his kilt. He'd never foxtrotted in a kilt before, but it seemed like a fun thing to do.

Teaching others a few more moves before the ball was something he was pleased to help the laird with as the festivities would soon be over for another year.

Sean made his son, Campbell, a hearty breakfast. Campbell was in his early thirties, a beemaster like his father, and lived in the large farmhouse. The spacious kitchen was the hub of the house.

Campbell had recently been renovating a cottage in a corner of one of their fields to make it his own home, but while it was the heart of winter, he mainly stayed with his father.

Joining Sean in their beekeeping and honey business in the autumn, Campbell was now dating

Beitris, known as Bee, an expert knitter and member of the local crafting bee. He had blond hair that swept up from his brow like a wave of burnished gold, green eyes with gold flecks, and enjoyed an outdoors lifestyle — rain, wind or snow. Wild weather came with the territory in his outdoor pursuits, but it had built a hardiness in Campbell despite his sophisticated appearance.

Sean, a successful businessman, was a fine looking man in his fifties with a flurry of light brown hair, and like Campbell, tall and fit. Sean was wealthy from his previous career in finance, and had then ventured into beemaster work. Together, they supplied local shops and online customers with their honey.

Campbell's career path had included architectural work, and although he'd made it his plan to work as a beemaster along with his father, he'd become involved in local building work and architectural design for Laurie and Gaven.

The laird had hired Campbell to help redesign new cabins for the castle's estate. And Campbell was involved in renovating Laurie's house, including adding a music recording studio. Local builders were hired for most of the building work for both projects. But Campbell was heavily involved too.

Sean poured two mugs of tea and sat down at the kitchen table to eat breakfast with Campbell. Breakfast included scrambled eggs, toast, grilled tomatoes, mushrooms and tattie scones.

'I've an excess of food that I bought in for Christmas,' said Sean. 'So I'm planning to cook a lavish roast dinner tonight with plenty of vegetables and roast tatties.'

'Oh, great. I'm heading up to Laurie's music studio this morning, but I'll make sure I'm back for a dinner like that.' Campbell smiled as he enjoyed his breakfast.

'I'm going to invite Muira and Sylvia for dinner,' said Sean. 'They close the sweet shop at five. I know the lassies have their craft night at the castle, but I plan to have the dinner ready sharp so they'll have time to eat it before going up to the castle.' He looked over at Campbell. 'Tell Bee she's welcome to join us. And extend the invitation to Laurie.'

Campbell nodded. 'I'll do that. He's supposed to be trying to finish songs for his new album, but I'll invite him to dinner.'

Sean started planning dinner for six. 'I'll make mashed tatties and roasties. Plenty of gravy, and I've a load of fresh vegetables that need cooked up, plus what's in the fridge. It'll go to waste if it's not used, and I'm happy to rustle up dinner for us.'

'I'll stop by Bee's cottage on my way to Laurie's house and tell her to join us for dinner tonight,' said Campbell. 'In this weather, with all the snow on the forest road up to the castle, I plan to drive her up to the craft night.'

'I was thinking the same about driving Muira there. Usually Sylvia drives them up, but my car can tackle the terrain better. I'll make the offer to drive them.'

14

'Aye, between us, we'll sort it out,' Campbell agreed. 'Let's see how many are going to turn up for dinner.'

Sean took out his phone. 'I'll call Muira right now.'

He explained his plan to Muira.

'Sylvia and I would love to have dinner with you, Sean. It'll save us having to rush and make something before it's time to go to the bee night.'

'Campbell's working on Laurie's recording studio today, so he's going to invite Laurie as well. And Bee will probably come for her dinner too,' Sean explained.

'We'll close the shop at five tonight and head to your house,' said Muira.

'I have a big tin of sweeties left over from Christmas, and a box of chocolates not missing many, so you don't need to bring anything except yourselves,' Sean told her.

'Okay, thanks for inviting us.'

Dinner agreed, the call ended on a happy note.

Sean topped up their mugs of tea and they continued to eat their breakfast.

'What's Laurie's music studio like?' said Sean. 'Is it a full recording studio set–up?'

'It is. The builders have added the sound proofing, and the equipment has been installed. Laurie plans to record most of his new songs in the studio here, rather than in the one he used in the city. It's a full recording facility with expensive equipment — a multi–track deck, lots of microphones, musical instruments. Laurie has it professionally kitted–out.'

'I like Laurie's songs, his music. And he seems a good match for Sylvia.'

Campbell scooped up a forkful of eggs and nodded. 'He's fair smitten with her.'

Sean smirked. 'I could say the same about you and Bee.'

Campbell couldn't deny it. 'And you and Muira.'

'There's a few budding romances in the village lately,' Sean admitted.

Campbell nodded and finished his breakfast. He stood up and put his warm jacket on. 'I'll see you later for dinner and I'll let you know if Laurie is coming too. I'm away to see Bee now. She'll want to join us for dinner I'm sure.'

Leaving the warmth of the kitchen, Campbell stepped out into the snow–covered garden and field surrounding the property. He got into his car and drove the short distance to Bee's cottage in one of the neighbouring fields.

Bee was living in her aunt and uncle's cottage, looking after it while they were away on business. It was the ideal setting to build up her knitting business, selling her knitted garments, and hand spun and dyed yarn, from her website. Originally from the Shetlands and then living in the Orkney islands too, she'd been knitting since she was a young girl and was a particularly fast knitter.

Campbell pulled up and parked in her garden and strode over the snow to her front door. He knocked and then went in, always welcome to drop by.

Following the rhythmic sound of her spinning wheel, he wandered through to where she had her knitting room set up. Shelves were stacked with all sorts of yarn, from double knit and Aran to fine lace weight. The lace shawls she knitted were some of her popular designs with customers locally and online.

Bee smiled when she saw the tall figure walk in. She was thirty, an attractive amber blonde with blue eyes and a petite build.

Campbell leaned down and kissed her. 'I'm on my way to work on Laurie's house. But Sean is making a tasty dinner for Muira and Sylvia, and he's invited you to join us. I'm going to invite Laurie too.'

'I'd love to go. I was thinking about wrapping up and heading down to the main street for groceries, so that would save me going out and I could get on with my spinning and knitting.'

'We know that you and the lassies are going to the crafting bee tonight,' said Campbell. 'But with the heavy snow on the forest road, Sean and I will drive you there and back.'

Bee smiled at him with warmth in her heart. 'What time should I come over for dinner?'

'Muira and Sylvia are shutting the sweet shop at five and heading round for dinner. Any time around five. I can pick you up on my way down.'

Bee brushed his offer aside. 'I'll walk over. It's not far and it'll give me some fresh air.'

'Wrap up warm,' Campbell advised her. 'It's a brisk morning, and it'll be twice as cold tonight.'

'I'll do that.' She leaned up and kissed him.

Leaving Bee to get on with her spinning, Campbell saw himself out, got into his car and headed up the forest road. There was a turnoff that led into the fields where Laurie's new house was situated. Everything from the distant hills and surrounding fields, separated with hedgerows, looked like a whiteout.

Campbell saw that the lights were on inside the house, indicating that the builders were already there and had started work early as planned.

He drove up and stepped out into the deep snow that covered the garden. The traditional house was a two–storey property, repainted white, and underneath the snow the roof was slate grey.

Two, tall evergreens stood as if on guard at the studio side of the house, creating a natural buffer against the elements.

The recording studio was an extension on one side. Campbell wasn't musically inclined, but even he liked the idea of having a recording studio right there as part of the house.

Most of the work had been done in the late summer, throughout the autumn and into the winter, slowing down only when the snow arrived early.

The interior decor was complete. The neutral tones stretched throughout the rooms. Beautiful watercolours adorned the walls, purchased from Oliver's art shop in the main street. Each large watercolour was painted by Oliver and depicted flowers and local scenery.

Laurie was rich and successful from his years in the music industry, and had poured a fair amount of money into having the property renovated. It was an open secret that Laurie was aiming to make this a home for himself and Sylvia. And gossip had been circulating since Christmas about Laurie planning to propose.

Some of the ladies from the crafting bee had suggested that Laurie was waiting until the spring to pop the question. No one knew for sure.

Sylvia tried to ignore the rumours and was happy to be dating Laurie. He'd shown her the house he'd bought before any renovations started, a brief visit, no more. Since then, she hadn't been back or participated in the redesigning as Laurie, Campbell and the local builders worked on it.

Laurie wanted to present it to her when the work was finished. In the interim, they spent time together in Laurie's cabin, especially after the crafting bee nights at the castle. And he went down to the sweet shop where she stayed in the cottage–style accommodation at the back of the shop.

So far, their dating routine was working well. Sylvia had become increasingly busy at the shop during the run–up to Christmas. And getting ready for the balls at the castle, involved with the crafting bee ladies sorting out their ballgowns and evening dresses for the dancing. Now, she was preparing to perform in the piano bar at the castle for the New Year event.

Songwriting took up a lot of Laurie's time, creating new material for his next album. So they'd both been busy.

Campbell smiled as he stepped into the entrance of the music recording studio. A token hallway had two sets of bagpipes, one hanging on either side, creating a silent Scottish musical welcome.

Laurie was already in the studio when Campbell walked in, having kicked the snow from his boots so as not to mess up the lovely new wood flooring. Parts of the studio were carpeted to help with the sound proofing, and Laurie had implemented his years of recording experience in various studios to amalgamate the best designs and layouts he'd worked in.

Cutting edge equipment was divided between two rooms for recording. A large glass panel separated one room from the master control room.

There were no windows, and areas were spotlighted with adjustable beams.

The sound proofing and subtle neutral tones of the decor created an atmosphere of silent style. Buffered from the noise of the outside world, Campbell imagined the new hit songs that would be written and played in the studio. In the quietude, he felt a sense of excitement.

Seeing the studio almost finished, Campbell gazed around at it and nodded. Three guitars hung on the walls, one acoustic and two electric. Others were on stands. The guitars bore marks where they'd been well–used and played during Laurie's past tours. Laurie had brought the guitars and the memories back home with him, and they were now part of the new future he was building.

A harp stood underneath a violin that was on the wall. The violin looked like it belonged to a vintage era. But it didn't look like it belonged to the past in Laurie's studio, and was part of the instrumental quality of the modern songs.

A Scottish fiddle that had played lively tunes at Christmastime hung alongside a gleaming saxophone. Even when silent, Campbell imagined he could hear the melodic tones of the sax. He knew Laurie played keyboards, piano and guitar, but it appeared that his abilities extended to several other instruments.

'This is impressive, Laurie. Seeing the studio now with all these lovely instruments in it.'

Laurie stood up from where he'd been sitting at the mixing desk. 'I rearranged the main studio area. Mainly where the instruments are located. I moved the keyboard over near the guitar stands to make room for something special.'

Campbell's eyes widened as he noticed what was behind him, tucked into a corner of the studio.

'It's arrived,' Laurie announced, gesturing to the beautiful baby grand piano.

CHAPTER TWO

Ian and Gaven ate breakfast in the guests' dining room at the castle. Seated at the laird's private table, they enjoyed bowls of chef's special porridge with creamy milk, and a pot of tea.

'I was hoping that you could teach an afternoon class of ballroom dancing, the foxtrot, like you did before Christmas when you taught the waltz,' Gaven explained. 'But I understand if you're busy.'

'I'd be happy to do this. I don't start rehearsals for my next show until January. I assume it would be the same as the lessons last time, held in the function room with an afternoon tea buffet,' said Ian.

'Yes, but just one afternoon before the New Year ball. Tomorrow afternoon if suitable. I'll put a notice up for guests. And the crafting bee is on tonight, so I'll invite the ladies along to the lesson too.'

This type of schedule had worked well before, and they agreed to go ahead with it.

Ian finished his porridge and looked thoughtful. 'What's on tomorrow night in the function room?'

'I have party nights every evening in the function room for guests. Dinner in the restaurant, or a buffet, and then music and dancing,' Gaven told him.

'Would you like to include ballroom dancing as part of the evening? I could come along and encourage guests to take part, especially those that had taken part in the afternoon dance lesson.'

Gaven nodded. 'Yes, that would be great.'

'We'd keep it light and fun. I could bring Rose as my dance partner. I'm teaching her the foxtrot, so this would encourage others to give it a go, especially with the right music.'

'Talk to Walter about whatever music you want,' said Gaven.

As they were talking, Walter escorted two new guests to their table in the dining room.

Gaven waved Walter over and explained what they were planning.

'I'll sort whatever music you need, Ian,' Walter confirmed cheerily.

Campbell sent Sean a message:
Laurie is coming to dinner, so is Bee.
Sean replied:
Dinner for six! See you later.

Campbell continued to work on the last adjustments needed to the patio of Laurie's house. It extended from the kitchen, doubling the dining area, and provided a wonderful view of the surrounding scenery.

Working on Laurie's property put Campbell in the mood to add the finishing touches to his own cottage. It was more or less done, and fit to live in, but with the Christmas rush, the renovations had become wrapped up in all the activity, and he wanted to find a few days when he could quietly make it perfect.

Bee had seen the cottage recently and loved it. He felt it was only a matter of time before he proposed to her. But the timing had to be right, not rushed, and he wasn't sure if it would seem too soon to pop the question. Laurie hadn't even proposed to Sylvia yet, and they'd been dating longer than he'd been dating Bee.

Mulling over these things was something he tended to do when involved in his architectural designs and building work. When he was dealing with the beehives he had to keep his focus one hundred percent on the bees. The hives had thrived during the warmer months, and although he hadn't joined his father to work with the bees until the autumn, he was looking forward to the spring and getting the hives ready again.

After breakfast with the laird at the castle, Ian drove back home and practised a few dances moves that he thought would be ideal to teach at the lesson the following afternoon, and for the party night.

He wrote down songs that would be suitable and sent a list to Walter.

It snowed again later in the day and he phoned Rose to offer to drive her up to the crafting bee night.

Looking out the window of her cottage at the heavy snow, Rose decided to take Ian up on his offer.

'Do you want to have dinner with me at the castle tonight?' Ian added to his original offer. 'Gaven was showing me chef's new menus and they look really tempting. I could pick you up early. We could have dinner and then you could go through to join the ladies for your crafting bee.'

'Okay, I'd like that. I'll be ready in time.'

'What are you working on today?' he said.

'Finishing one quilt and starting to piece together another one. I can get a lot of quilting done on a snow day like this. And I'll take my quilting to the bee night.'

'I've been planning the dance lesson. I'll tell you all about it tonight.'

After the call, Rose continued to work at her sewing machine, finishing a quilt she'd designed using a new range of fabric she'd bought from Aileen's quilt shop in the main street. Aileen was an expert quilter and her shop sold a lovely range of quilting weight cotton and other fabrics. Many of the crafting bee members bought their fabric from Aileen.

Rose loved being part of the local crafting community, and was hopeful of building her small business from her cottage. She'd started her business a few years ago while she was studying textile design and living in Edinburgh, creating and selling full–size quilts to smaller items including stylish bags and appliqué quilted cushion covers.

Etta, one of the key members of the crafting bee had welcomed Rose into the bee, and this extended to social events and helping each other make dresses to wear to the various parties and functions that were a regular part of life in the village.

Glancing out the window at the snow fluttering by, Rose continued to quilt until it was time to get ready for dinner with Ian.

The lights shone from the windows of Rose's cottage as Ian pulled up and stepped out of his car. The night sky was a dark, inky blue and sprinkled with stars. The cold air had a crispness to it.

Rose was ready, warmly dressed in her coat, cords and boots, and wearing a white jumper. Her hair hung in chestnut waves around the collar of her coat. She grabbed her craft bag and hurried out, smiling at Ian.

He leaned down and kissed her. The loving breath from their kiss rose up into the icy air.

They quickly got into the warmth of the car.

'I've booked a table for us,' he said, turning up the heater and driving off, taking his time to navigate the narrow road leading down to the loch. Everything was thick with fresh snow.

The grass around the edges of the loch glistened in the nightglow.

'The loch looks beautiful,' said Rose, looking out the window as they drove by.

Ian nodded. 'The whole countryside is gorgeous in winter. According to Gaven, the snow usually lasts until the end of January, sometimes longer.'

'It'll still be a snowscape then when you leave to start rehearsals for the new show.' Her comment hung in the air between them. She didn't mean to bring the conversation around to Ian leaving, and wished she hadn't brought it up.

'You know that I'll be driving back and forth from Edinburgh during rehearsals and often when I'm performing in the show,' he said, feeling the need to reassure her.

'Yes, and I'll come and enjoy the odd day in Edinburgh when you're extra busy with matinee performances and evening shows in the theatre.'

'And go round the shops in the city,' he said, sounding chirpy. 'We'll have lunch and dinner there too. It'll be fun.'

Rose smiled at him. 'I always have fun when I'm with you, Ian.'

'Even when I'm trying to teach you the foxtrot?'

'I enjoy a challenge, and it's such an elegant dance. I will learn to dance it properly.'

'You've improved immensely,' he insisted.

Ian navigated the car up the forest road as they continued to chat.

'What dances are you teaching at the castle this time?'

'An afternoon of foxtrot.'

'I thought you'd be teaching people how to waltz.'

'I did that last time. The winter and Christmas balls were wonderful for waltzing. But Gaven says that the New Year ball is a mix of ceilidh dancing, lots of reels and jigs, and ballroom dancing, waltzing mainly, but he's listed foxtrot too. I'd love to encourage guests to foxtrot.'

'It sounds like a lively evening to ring in the New Year.'

'Yes, and I suggested to Gaven that I'd take part in one of the party nights leading up to the ball. So I'll teach in the afternoon tomorrow, and then help to liven things up with dancing in the evening.'

Rose blinked. 'There's a dance tomorrow night at the castle?'

Ian smiled and nodded. 'There are party nights every evening on the run–up to the ball, and I thought it would be fun to take part. That's what I wanted to talk to you about. I hope you'll come with me tomorrow night.'

Rose smiled. 'Okay. What should I wear? Is it informal or glam?'

'An evening dress, or one of your lovely tea dresses. And your dancing shoes.'

Rose started to think what dress she'd wear.

'Gaven is extending the afternoon lesson to the crafting bee ladies as well as guests,' Ian told her. 'He expects most of them will join in. Would you like to come along?'

'Yes, especially as the other ladies will be joining in.'

'It'll give you a chance to practise your foxtrot.'

Ian drove up to the castle. The windows were all lit up, including the turret, the private accommodation where Gaven lived.

Snow covered the extensive gardens and one of the large trees outside the castle was decorated with Christmas lights.

Ian parked near the front entrance. A welcoming glow poured out on to the snow.

He wrapped his arm around Rose as they hurried into reception.

Jessy and Walter were working in reception and smiled in welcoming.

'Are you going to the crafting bee tonight?' Jessy said to Rose.

Rose held up her craft bag. 'Yes, I'll be there after dinner.'

Ian read the notices that were pinned up advertising the dance lesson.

'Guests have shown an interest already,' Walter told Ian. 'You'll have a busy class.'

'They're excited about the dancing in the evening too,' Jessy added.

Ian smiled and read the information that was included on the notices. 'I see that Gaven has listed some of the party night dances — including the foxtrot.'

Jessy nodded enthusiastically. 'Waltzing is great, and we all enjoyed learning that, but it'll be exciting to try other dances.'

'I hope they'll find it a fun class,' said Ian.

'I'm sure they will,' Jessy told him.

'I'll show you to your table,' Walter said and led Rose and Ian through to the restaurant. 'I've got your dance music all sorted out for you,' he told Ian.

'Thanks, Walter. And are you coming along to the lesson or the dancing in the evening?'

'I'll be buzzing around at both,' said Walter, taking their coats as they were seated at their table.

A member of the catering staff handed Ian and Rose menus.

'Chef's new menus are so tempting,' Walter told them, and then took their coats through to the cloakroom in reception while they read the selection. A few of the items included Sean and Campbell's honey.

'The hearty roast dinner with all the trimmings — puff pastry and roast potatoes sounds tasty,' Ian said to Rose. 'I'll have that.'

Rose agreed. 'I won't need a starter. The main course is quite substantial.'

Ian smiled over at her. 'Pudding?'

Rose eyed the selection. 'Oh, yes. Chef's chocolate pudding.'

Ian nodded, smiled, closed his menu and ordered their dinner.

Sean had planned to serve the dinner in the living room at the dining table. But everyone arrived in a flurry of cheery activity within minutes of each other, and settled themselves down at the large wooden table in the kitchen, so Sean served dinner for six there.

The warmth of the oven heated the spacious kitchen, and everyone seemed happy to gather around together.

Campbell had driven Laurie down after finishing the work at the house and studio, and planned to give the singer a lift back up to the castle after dinner along with the ladies. It was the first time Laurie had been to Sean's house.

Laurie wore jeans and a Fair Isle jumper he'd bought from Etta. She'd knitted it in shades of grey. It had become his favourite new jumper.

Campbell wore a blue cable knit jumper that Bee had knitted for him. The blue matched his jeans.

Bee had knitted a classic cream Aran jumper for Sean, and he'd teamed it with a pair of dark grey winter trousers.

Muira was wearing a skirt, top and a lilac cardigan she'd knitted, while Sylvia had changed into a pair of slim–fitting dark cords that she teamed with a pink jumper Muira had knitted. Pretty but practical for dinner followed by the crafting bee.

As a professional knitter, Bee was always wearing the items she knitted herself, but instead of opting for a jumper or cardigan, she wore a white, long–sleeve blouse with a knitted top, like a sleeveless jumper, in shades of blue. It was one of her own designs. Ink blue velvet trousers completed her outfit. Her knitted vests and waistcoats were currently popular with her customers for the winter months.

Bee glanced around, noting that everyone was wearing something that had been hand knitted.

Laurie took in the decor, particularly the items that had a bee theme. He smiled at the needle felted bumblebee sitting on a shelf. 'I like the wee nods to your beemaster work.'

Sean put on a set of quilted oven gloves that were handmade from a bee print fabric. 'The crafting bee ladies made me a welcoming basket when I arrived here with everything from the oven gloves to a knitted tea cosy and egg cosies. All handmade with a bee theme.' He gestured to the felted bee. 'Muira recently gave me the needle felted bee. It's a white–tailed bumblebee. I love it.'

Muira smiled and blushed a little.

'I like things like that,' said Laurie.

Muira and Bee exchanged a knowing look. The crafting bee ladies had been making items for Laurie, housewarming gifts, with a musical theme.

Sean checked the roast in the oven and the tray of potatoes he had sizzling nicely. 'Dinner's ready.'

A pile of plates and cutlery were on the dresser and Campbell began to set the table. Everyone helped in small ways and within minutes they were all seated and tucking into the delicious dinner.

Sean had cooked up a load of fresh vegetables including roast parsnips and mashed turnip and carrots.

Laurie scooped up a forkful of the turnip mix. 'I love neeps and carrot.'

'I like to make it at New Year too,' said Sean. 'But I had lots of vegetables left from overstocking for Christmas.'

'I had lunch at the castle's restaurant recently and the new menu is great,' said Laurie. 'There's a special menu for Hogmanay and the New Year. I'll miss just popping over for my meals when I move into my house.'

Campbell cut into one of the roasties. 'That's all the work done,' he announced with a smile.

Laurie was sitting opposite and gave him a look.

'What I mean is,' Campbell corrected himself. 'My work is done there.' He'd forgotten that Laurie didn't want to announce that the house was finished just yet. It was, but he had something special planned. He didn't elaborate, but Campbell surmised it involved Sylvia. And the new baby grand piano in the music studio was to be kept a secret.

'When will the house be finished?' Sylvia said, smiling pleasantly. Her green eyes sparkled with curiosity. She was keen to see it, but as Laurie hadn't invited her to see the progress on the house, she didn't push the issue. He'd invite her in his own good time, she'd told herself.

'Soon.' Laurie's one word reply was accompanied with a tense smile.

Sean picked up on the tension. 'How is your songwriting coming along? I enjoyed your last album.'

The tension lifted as Laurie revealed that he was still writing songs for the new album. 'I've got a couple of new melodies playing in my head. I just need the lyrics to make the songs become something that I'm happy with. Nearly there with the majority of the songs though. I'm finding that I write well living here in the Highlands.'

'The new song you sang in the main street at Christmastime was a winner,' said Muira.

'We were all impressed, and surprised that you let us hear it first,' Sylvia added.

'It seemed appropriate,' Laurie admitted. 'The timing felt right. Christmas. Everyone gathered in the main street that night. The whole atmosphere.'

'It was a grand night,' said Sean. 'And I'm looking forward to the New Year ball at the castle.' He glanced at Muira sitting beside him. 'Another special night for us.'

'The ball will be a lovely way to celebrate Hogmanay,' Muira agreed, smiling at Sean.

'My first New Year here.' Campbell looked at Bee and Laurie. 'A first for a few of us.'

'I've been here for three years, but I kept myself to myself for most of that time,' Sean admitted. 'Now that Campbell's here, and Muira and I are together, it feels like a fresh start.'

Campbell raised his teacup in a cheers. 'To happy and prosperous new beginnings for all of us.'

Everyone raised their cups in a tea toast.

As the chatter continued and they enjoyed their dinner, Laurie felt his heart long to make a future with Sylvia.

'You've a fair bit of land around this lovely farmhouse,' Laurie commented to Sean.

'This is our main field for the bees, the hives,' Sean explained. 'But we're planning to make the most of the other fields too.'

'I noticed a white–painted cottage in the far corner. Is that the one you were renovating?' Laurie said to Campbell.

'It is. I've finished rebuilding the outside, and the interior decor is done now too,' said Campbell. 'I'm planning to move into it permanently when the weather is a wee bit milder.' Campbell glanced at Bee. He had lots of other plans, all involving her. He'd painted the kitchen a light sky blue for her. But at this hectic time of year, he wanted the seasonal celebrations to calm down before he made plans to settle down with Bee. 'Come over one day and I'll show you the cottage,' he said to Laurie.

'I'll do that,' Laurie confirmed.

'I intend to cultivate the garden in the spring.' Campbell's beemaster work included having an excellent knowledge of plants and flowers.

'Underneath the snow, there's a carpet of heather covering parts of our fields,' Sean added. 'And the flowers have a wild beauty.'

'The garden around your house has the potential to be lovely,' Campbell told Laurie.

'I'm not a gardener, but I intend to learn,' said Laurie. 'I want my house to feel like a real home, and potter around the garden in my spare time.'

'Since I moved into the cottage part of the sweet shop, I've been trying to learn gardening,' Sylvia told them. Then she smiled. 'But the most I've done is pot some plants outside the kitchen and add twinkle lights so I can sit outside in the evenings and relax.'

Laurie reacted, taking this in, thinking what to add to his garden that Sylvia would like. Certainly twinkle lights.

Then Sylvia revealed news that made Laurie's world tilt.

'I've had word that a sweetie–making course I'd been thinking about months ago will be available soon.' Sylvia glanced at Muira. 'Though I'm not sure that I want or need to go on the course now. I love working at the shop and I'm already making my own recipes for sweets and chocolate.' And she'd become involved in playing the piano again after years of giving it up in favour of a career in baking and sweets.

Muira sighed heavily. Her niece had told her this earlier at the shop. 'I'd never want to influence you, Sylvia, but I don't know what else you could learn from this course that would benefit you. Didn't you say the course was geared towards how to set up your own sweet shop or patisserie rather than learning new recipes and techniques.'

'Yes,' said Sylvia. 'At the time I didn't know I'd be coming to settle here, or for how long I'd be working with you.'

Laurie tried to keep his voice steady. 'When does the course start?'

'The second week in January. It's in the city,' said Sylvia.

'So you'd be travelling from the village to the city during the course?' Laurie surmised.

Sylvia shook her head. 'No, it's not Edinburgh. It's Glasgow. A four–month course. I'd need to find a flat in Glasgow while I was away.'

Laurie felt his world tilt even more.

Sylvia shrugged, not knowing how deeply this affected him. 'I haven't made any plans to go on the course yet. I probably won't go.'

Probably gave Laurie hope, but it still wasn't complete assurance. In the back of his mind, he remembered Sylvia mentioning the course, but then everything changed and she'd become involved in his music. Playing piano on some of the tracks. He'd assumed they'd work together. Be together.

No one at the table seemed to pick up on Laurie's turmoil, except Sean, but he kept his comments to himself, waiting on a private moment to chat to Laurie.

Sean stood up, and started to clear the dinner plates. 'Anyone for pudding?'

Several sets of eager hands helped to clear the plates away and get the pudding dishes and spoons ready.

Everyone was up for pudding.

A traditional Christmas pudding, rich with raisins, sultanas, cinnamon, nutmeg and glacé cherries, sat on the kitchen dresser, ready to be served up and have custard or cream poured over it. Maybe even a bit of both.

CHAPTER THREE

Gaven came out of his office behind the reception desk and sighed heavily. 'There are no pipers available now,' he said to Walter and Jessy. 'They're all booked to play at New Year parties.'

It was part of the traditional celebration to have a piper play the bagpipes at the castle to ring in the New Year. The one they'd booked had to cancel and Gaven tried to find a replacement.

'I'll set up some bagpipe music to play outside the castle,' Walter suggested. 'We have to have something for the midnight chimes.'

Gaven nodded, but the disappointment weighed heavily on his shoulders. They always had a piper play live. It was a long–standing tradition. Guests expected to hear the bagpipes and see the piper outside the castle playing in the snow. It had been advertised as part of the New Year ball's itinerary. 'Thank you, Walter.'

'I don't know anyone local that could step in and play,' said Jessy.

Gaven shrugged. 'There's no one that plays the pipes.'

Walter eyed Gaven. 'Except you.'

Gaven blinked. 'I haven't played in years. I don't even have a set of bagpipes.'

Out of options, they settled for Walter's solution to the predicament.

Sean drove Muira, Sylvia and Laurie up the forest road to the castle after dinner. Campbell followed in his car with Bee.

They could see the lights shining from the castle in the distance.

Laurie hadn't found a private moment to talk to Sylvia about her course, though he wasn't sure what to say. He certainly didn't want to persuade her to give up the course if it was what she wanted, but his stomach was still churning at the thought of her leaving the village and moving away, even if it was only for a few months.

The two cars pulled up outside the castle and as they all got out, Sean smiled at Laurie.

'Are you coming in with us, Laurie, or heading to your cabin?'

Laurie hesitated. He hadn't considered he'd join them. Usually while Sylvia attended the crafting bee nights, he'd be in his cabin and she'd pop in to see him afterwards. 'I should probably get back to my cabin and get on with my songwriting.'

Sylvia, Muira and Bee hurried inside out of the cold carrying their craft bags.

Sean and Campbell were about to follow them, when Laurie reconsidered.

'I'll come in for a wee while,' said Laurie.

They all headed inside to the reception. The restaurant and guests' dining room were busy.

Jessy beckoned to Sylvia, Muira and Bee from the doorway of the function room. They weren't late, but often the crafting bee evenings started early.

'Come away in,' Jessy called to them. 'Gaven's inviting us to join in Ian's dance class tomorrow afternoon.'

Leaving Sean, Campbell and Laurie in reception, the ladies hurried through to the crafting bee.

'Are you staying to take the lassies home after their bee night?' Walter said to them.

'Yes,' Campbell told him. 'But we've had dinner.'

'Just as well,' Walter remarked. 'Folk are eager to try chef's new menu. It's a busy evening, but the piano bar is quieter. Find yourselves a seat through there. Would you like a drink or tea?'

'Tea for Campbell and me,' said Sean. 'What about you, Laurie?'

'I'll have tea,' said Laurie, not intending to stay for long.

'Did someone say tea?' Ian emerged from the function room, leaving Gaven to continue chatting to the ladies.

After having dinner with Ian, Rose had gone through to join in the crafting, and Ian had accompanied Gaven to help explain what was planned for the dancing lesson.

'We're going through to the piano bar,' Sean said to Ian. 'You're welcome to join us.'

Laurie read the notices about the dance lesson and party nights, and as the men chatted for a few moments in reception, Walter shrugged on his warm jacket, woollen hat and put on a pair of thick gloves. He seemed in a rush to wrap up and hurry outside, unhooking a bunch of keys from behind the desk.

'Is that you off home now, Walter?' Sean said to him.

'Nah, I'm away to set off fireworks,' Walter explained. 'If you hear whizzing and whooshing noises from outside, don't worry. It's just me causing a ruckus.'

'Fireworks?' Sean frowned. 'What are you up to?'

The other men listened while Walter explained. 'I'm testing some of the fireworks for the New Year ball celebration. We set them off at midnight every year. I don't want to take a chance with them because we've already had a disappointment. Our piper had to cancel and we've no one to play the bagpipes. Gaven used to play, but he doesn't even have a set of bagpipes and he hasn't played in years. So I need to make sure the firework display goes according to plan.'

'Where are the fireworks?' said Sean.

'I've got them stored in the shed. I'll light a few to check they're okay.' Walter started to head out.

'Do you need a hand?' Sean offered.

Campbell stepped forward too. 'I've handled fireworks before.'

Walter looked keen to have their help. 'If you're up for it, yes. But it's a freezing night.'

All of them, except Ian, were still wearing their warm jackets.

'I'll give you a hand,' Laurie said, willing to tackle the task.

'Let me grab my jacket,' Ian told them. 'I'll come with you.' He hurried through to the cloakroom, put his jacket and boots on, and hurried outside with the others into the snowy night.

Campbell dug out his woollen gloves from his jacket pockets and put them on. Bee had knitted them for him.

All of the men buttoned up and wore hats and gloves if they had them. Their boots crunched through the snow as they followed Walter to the back of the castle. Lights shone from the function room windows out on to the snow, but the five figures walked by unnoticed by the ladies inside or Gaven. The laird was still telling them about the dancing lesson and party night, and chatting to them about the forthcoming ball.

Laurie saw Sylvia standing beside Penny looking at a beautiful yellow evening dress. The other ladies were listening to Gaven while working on their crafts. The bee was a hive of activity, and three of the ladies were seated at sewing machines making quilts.

Their tables and chairs were set up on one side of the large function room that had a dance floor where the party celebrations were held. A roaring fire flickered in the hearth and the Christmas decorations added festive glitter to the room.

Campbell was tempted to chap on one of the glass patio doors and wave in to Bee, but thought better of it, not wanting to disturb their evening, or cause the ladies to be concerned about what they were about to do. Campbell had no qualms about helping Walter set off a few test fireworks. He was quite looking forward to it. So were the others, and they had a sense of mischief and excitement about their snowy night adventure.

Sean noticed Muira knitting and chatting to the other ladies and Gaven. Engrossed in this, she didn't see him skulk by.

Ian was up for taking part in whatever Walter was planning. It felt invigorating being out in the snow. He saw Rose sewing a cushion cover, sitting with Etta and Jessy, but like the other men, Ian hurried by in stealth mode.

'I had a lovely dinner with Ian,' Rose said to Jessy and Etta. 'Ian plans to relax in the piano bar while I'm here at the bee. Then he'll drive me home.'

'The castle's restaurants are busy tonight,' said Jessy. 'Sean, Campbell and Laurie are probably relaxing in the piano bar with Ian.'

Muira nodded. 'Yes, Sean often has a cup of tea there while I'm here.'

The sewing machines whirred in the background as members worked on their quilts.

Gaven made sure the ladies had everything they needed for their evening. 'As this is the last crafting bee night before the New Year, chef's planning to serve up a few tasty treats along with your usual scones and tea.'

The ladies thanked Gaven. He went to walk away, but Etta had a question for him.

'Do we need partners for the dance lesson like we did before?' Etta was in her fifties with silvery blonde hair and was working on a cable knit jumper. She lived in a cottage by the loch, worked from home, and sold her knitting locally and online from her website.

43

'Ian says that the lesson will be like the last ones. Bring a partner if you can so you can practise dancing with them,' said Gaven. 'But it's not necessary as people will be paired up to learn the foxtrot. And Walter will be on hand, and I'll be there as well.' Gaven then left them to get on with their crafting and discuss their dance plans.

Penny gave Sylvia the dress she'd brought for her. 'I'm sure Neil will come with me. He enjoyed the dancing before.' Penny was in her thirties and wore her blonde hair up in a chignon. She took out her phone to message Neil.

Aileen, owner of the quilt shop in the main street, was similar in age to Penny, and her dark brown hair was swept up at the sides with clasps. The style emphasised her hazel eyes and porcelain complexion. Aileen sent a message to her boyfriend, Fyn, the flower shop owner. 'I'll see if Fyn will join in again.' They'd known each other for a while and started dating in the summertime.

'Will you be dancing with Ian?' Etta said to Rose.

Rose continued working on the appliqué cushion she was stitching. 'Probably. Ian invited me to come to the lesson and the dance party at night. I've been learning the foxtrot. I haven't got the hang of it yet, but it's a lovely dance to learn.'

Robin, a textile artist and knitwear model, in her early thirties, had long strawberry blonde hair, and was engaged to Oliver the artist. She put her sewing aside and messaged him about the dance lesson.

Oliver replied to Robin:
I'm happy to go with you.

Oliver had been working on the illustrations for one of his new books in his art shop. He lived in stylish accommodation above the shop, and was in his thirties, fine featured with dark brown hair and green eyes. Oliver planned to close his art shop the following afternoon so he could attend the lesson with Robin.

Penny received a message from Neil:

Yes, I'll go. I'd like to learn more dancing from Ian.

Neil's goldwork designs, especially his rings, were exclusive and exquisite. He was in his thirties, had light brown hair and pale aqua blue eyes. He invariably wore classic clothes, suits, shirts, ties, waistcoats, and like Ian, Neil didn't do casual.

Several of the ladies received replies confirming they had partners for the dance lesson or the dance party.

'Sean's a great dancer,' said Muira, continuing to knit her cardigan. 'He's what I would call a competent social dancer. I love dancing with him. Sean will want to go.'

'We'll tell Sean and Campbell later,' said Bee, busily knitting a Fair Isle jumper.

'I'll tell Laurie later too,' Sylvia added, admiring the evening dress that Penny had altered for her.

Nothing got past chef without him noticing. As Walter and the others trudged by the kitchen windows, the back door burst open and chef peered out into the night. Lamps lit parts of the castle's exterior, but everything was cast in shadows and pockets of light.

Walter expected chef to challenge what they were up to. But instead, chef called over to Sean and Campbell.

'I need more honey!' Chef's urgent tone sounded clear in the night air.

'I'll drop off an order first thing in the morning,' Sean called back.

Chef stuck his thumb up. 'Cheers!' Then he closed the door and let them get on with their mischief.

Walter looked relieved and they continued on to the back of one of the storerooms. He jangled the set of keys and unlocked the door. 'Come on in. Pick up a torch or a lantern. We'll need plenty of light to see what we're doing.'

They followed Walter inside, all kicking the snow from their boots.

'There are lanterns over here.' Walter pointed to shelves stacked with various types of outdoor lanterns. 'We use them for wedding receptions, mainly during the spring and summer evenings. And for other events. Or for evenings when we take the guests for a wee evening trek through the estate.'

The men picked up a lantern each and lit them.

Walter grabbed a large torch and handed another two torches to Sean and Campbell.

'Right, that should do us,' Walter announced and led them back outside. Holding up one of the lanterns to lead the way, he headed towards a large shed that was hidden by trees and greenery at the rear of the castle. 'The shed is over here.'

'What type of fireworks have you got?' Campbell called to Walter.

'What have I not got,' Walter replied with a chuckle.

Campbell and the others laughed.

'I ordered our usual supply,' Walter explained. 'But I added a few new ones to try this year.'

Walter's keys jangled again as he fished out the one to open the shed door.

Snow was packed around the edges of the shed door, but Campbell helped him open it while Sean and the others held up the lanterns.

Shining a torch inside the wooden shed, Walter went in and sat his lantern down on the workbench. The glow illuminated everything. Boxes of fireworks sat on the bench and were stacked neatly in a corner. The shed was dry and well kept.

The men stepped inside and Campbell was particularly keen to see the range of tools for gardening and handyman work that Walter had hanging up tidily.

'Nice shed and some handy tools,' Campbell said to Walter.

Walter glanced around. 'I like my shed. It's a cosy nook to coorie in.'

Laurie peered into the back of the shed. 'Is that a sledge you've got stashed?'

Walter shone the torch near the sledge, highlighting that there were three of them piled up. 'Three sledges. I've been working on them. There are other sledges in the store for the guests to use. I'll show you on the way back. But these are old–fashioned sledges that I've had for years. They go like the wind if you're daring enough to give them a try.'

'I'm up for it,' Laurie said, going over and having a look at the sledges. 'I used to love going sledging when I was a boy, and sometimes on holiday. I never seem to have time for things like that these days.'

'You've got to make time for the things you miss,' said Walter. 'I didn't tell Gaven, but when we had the first snow before Christmas, I enjoyed whizzing doon one of the wee slopes in the forest. I had a great time.'

'Do you think we could have a go while we're all here?' said Sean. 'The lassies are busy with their crafting.'

'Aye, let's test a firework from each of the new boxes,' Walter suggested. 'Then we'll go night sledging.'

Laughter and cheery chatter filled the shed as the men worked together to set up the fireworks outside where it was safe to set them off.

'I've done this for years,' Walter assured them. 'But if you could help me position them safely, that would be great.'

Trudging through the snow to where Walter wanted to set them up, the men got ready to light the first firework.

'I like to colour coordinate the fireworks display,' Walter explained. 'I'm not sure if this is gold, blue or multi–coloured.' He got set to light it. 'Stand well back.'

'What happens if the guests hear or see the fireworks?' Ian said to Walter.

'Ach, there's so much music, chatter and everything going on tonight, they'll never know,' said Walter, brushing aside any concerns. 'This area is private so guests are well out of the way, and no one will be venturing out on a freezing night like this, especially as they'll be having their dinner. We'll be done in a few minutes, thanks to you all helping.'

The men stepped back as Walter used a long tapering device to light the fireworks.

Muira blinked. 'Was that a shooting star in the sky?' From where she was sitting knitting, she had a view outside the function room, but the lights from inside made it difficult to see the dark night sky clearly.

'There are always shooting stars at this time of year,' Jessy remarked. 'Especially when it's been snowing.'

'Oh, there's another one.' This time it was Rose that saw it. 'It had a blue glow.'

'Probably the nightglow,' Jessy assessed.

The other ladies nodded.

None of them stopped their crafting to go over to peer out, and instead decided to make wishes from where they were seated sewing and knitting.

Bee's face lit up with a smile. 'That star had a gold glittery tail. I'm wishing for a prosperous New Year for all of us.'

They agreed, and joined in with Bee's wish.

'Are we supposed to say what we're wishing for?' Penny said to them.

'Yes,' said Etta. 'When we're all wishing on stars together.'

Sylvia saw the final one shooting across the sky. 'Oh, that one is a gorgeous pink sparkly one.' She closed her eyes and made a wish. 'I'm wishing for romance.'

'To romance!' the ladies said in unison.

As that was the last of the starry display, the ladies got on with their crafting.

Minutes later, a silver trolley with their tea, scones, strawberry jam, and tasty treats from chef was wheeled through and served up by a member of staff.

Jessy and Muira got up to help serve the tea, delicious cake and savoury pastries.

'Chef's spoiling us tonight,' Etta remarked, tucking into a flaky cheese pastry.

Sylvia bit into a white chocolate cupcake that was swirled with buttercream. 'I love chef's chocolate cakes,' she mumbled.

'I can never resist a snowball.' Muira put one of the Scottish snowball cakes on a plate and grabbed a napkin, hoping to contain the coconut and crumbs.

Bee selected a savoury vol–au–vent. 'Campbell and the other men don't know what they're missing.'

The ladies giggled and enjoyed their special tea break.

Walter wrote the colours and effects of the fireworks on a notepad in the shed. 'All sorted. Those will work well with our usual display. Thanks for your help, lads.'

Eager faces smiled at him.

'Okay, select a sledge and let's go.'

Laurie lifted one, and seemed to be partnered with Ian.

Sean and Campbell hoisted the other two sledges up, carried them outside and sat them down on the snow. There was no one else around and they had the whole snowscape to themselves.

Walter locked the shed and tucked the keys in his jacket pocket.

'We'll head for the first slope over there.' Walter held his lantern aloft and led the way to a clearing within the forest that surrounded the estate.

Laurie had his own technique for getting there faster, and was pushing off from the sledge, using the strength in his legs to create momentum across the flat of the snow.

Campbell and Sean joined in, making it a friendly race between the three of them.

Walter and Ian had to run to keep up, carrying their lanterns.

The men's laughter rang out in the clear, cold air as they got ready to hit the wee slopes for a night of boisterous adventure.

CHAPTER FOUR

'No, Walter, No!' Campbell shouted, seeing Walter jump in a sledge and steer it towards a slope where the snow looked particularly deep and hard to navigate.

Walter's laughter resonated in the icy air as he whizzed past Campbell and Sean, leaving Laurie and Ian behind at the top of the slope.

Campbell and Sean trudged through the snow as fast as they could, urging Walter to slow down, while Laurie and Ian charged after him in their sledges. They'd all placed their lanterns at the edges of the slope to light the route, and hung a couple of them from low–hanging tree branches while they took turns each on the three sledges.

Eager to show them his sledging prowess, Walter's enthusiasm got the better of him. As he approached a bank of snow at speed, the others winced as he took off and ended up face planting in it. His sledge slid on a short distance, leaving Walter spluttering in the snow.

Laurie and Ian were the first to slide to a halt a safe distance from the snow banking. They jumped off their sledges and hurried to help Walter. Sean and Campbell arrived moments later.

Amid the spluttering, Walter was laughing and stood up, brushing the snow from his clothes.

The others, now seeing that Walter was fine from taking a tumble into the snow, joined in the laughter.

'You're a scallywag!' Sean chided Walter.

Walter smiled. 'Can I pretend that was intentional?' he joked.

'Aye, right,' said Campbell, shaking his head at him.

The laughter continued, and so did a few more runs of sledging, without any further daring antics from Walter.

But on the final run, Sean and Campbell teamed up on one sledge, with Laurie and Ian on a second one, while Walter had the third one to himself.

'Ready, steady...go!' Walter shouted.

And off they went, tearing down the long slope that levelled out into a flat surface of thick snow.

Sean, Campbell, Laurie and Ian all punched the air as the challenge resulted in the nearest to a draw they could've hoped for.

Walter slid to a halt moments later. 'That looked like a tie for the win.'

The others agreed, and then collected their lanterns. Taking their sledges with them, they trudged back to the shed.

Helping Walter to brush the snow off the sledges, the men tidied them away in the shed.

Walter locked the shed door, and checked the time. 'The crafting bee will still be in full swing, but we'll take a shortcut through the storeroom rather than make an entrance through reception.'

Taking Walter's surreptitious suggestion, they all headed into the storeroom, but encountered chef while they were taking their jackets off and brushing the telltale snow from themselves.

'Up to no good, eh?' Chef looked at them with an accusing smile. His hat was tilted at a jaunty angle, an indication that it had been another busy night of cooking in the kitchen.

'The lads were helping me test the fireworks,' said Walter. Not a lie, but not entirely the truth.

Chef shook his head at them. 'I know fine what you rascals were up to. Away through to the piano bar. I'll organise mugs of hot chocolate for you.'

Smiling their thanks to chef, the men made their way through the storeroom to the piano bar.

Walter bundled their jackets up. 'I'll stash these in the cloakroom. Go and sit yourselves down at a table.'

The four men sat at a table near the baby grand piano in a corner of the room. The dark wood of the piano looked like glass. The piano was available for guests to play, though few had the capability, so it was always a treat when Sylvia played on special evenings. Laurie could play, but he wasn't as skilled as Sylvia.

The piano bar was a new addition to the castle's facilities. It had tables arranged around the room, and each one had a small lamp to give an atmospheric glow. Chandeliers sparkled overhead. The Art Deco bar had a mirrored finish, and the vintage design added to the old–fashioned styling of the piano bar.

Three paintings by Oliver hung on the walls, depicting a classic black grand piano, a decorative cocktail glass, and an Art Deco style couple dancing. The paintings added to the decor and relaxing ambiance.

Laurie had been thinking about Gaven's predicament, and when Walter came back through to check that they were settled, he brought up the subject.

'If Gaven had a set of bagpipes, could he play them?' Laurie said to Walter.

'Aye, I suppose he could,' Walter confirmed. 'He says he's out of practise, but he used to be a fine piper. Learned when he was a boy.'

'I have two sets of bagpipes in my music studio,' Laurie told him.

Walter's eyes lit up with hope. 'You should tell Gaven. He's busy with guests in the restaurant, but he'll be back in reception soon.'

'Do you play the bagpipes?' Ian said to Laurie.

'I do, though I'm in the same situation as Gaven,' Laurie admitted. 'I learned years ago, but I rarely play these days. I'm well out of practise too.' He looked at Walter. 'What songs do your pipers usually play to ring in the New Year?'

Walter listed off three main songs. 'But any tune you could play would be better than me rigging up music outside.'

Laurie went over to the piano and sat down on the stool. Knowing the songs, Laurie began playing them, reminding himself of the tunes, and wondering if he could remember how to play the bagpipes.

Chef wheeled through a silver trolley and served up five mugs of hot chocolate. 'This will heat you up from your sledging and skulduggery.'

The men smiled guiltily.

Walter lifted up a mug, though he'd no intention of sitting down and planned to get back to reception.

Chef hurried away again.

As chef left, a few of the bee ladies peered in, hearing Laurie playing the piano.

'Yes, they've been relaxing in the piano bar,' Jessy whispered, confirming what they'd thought earlier about Sean, Campbell, Ian and Laurie.

Sylvia, Muira, Bee and Rose peered in.

'Laurie plays the piano beautifully,' Bee murmured.

The other ladies agreed.

'They're having hot chocolate by the looks of it,' Rose said, keeping her voice down.

'We'll not disturb them,' whispered Muira.

Nodding to each other, the ladies disappeared back through to the function room to get on with their crafting.

Laurie moved on to playing one of the other songs Walter had mentioned. Another traditional number he knew from yesteryear.

'Ah, it's you, Laurie,' Gaven announced striding into the piano bar. 'I heard someone playing the piano. I wondered if it was Sylvia. That's one of the traditional songs we play at New Year.'

'I told Laurie about the songs,' said Walter. 'And about our current predicament.'

'Walter explained about you not having a piper for the ball,' said Laurie.

Gaven sighed and nodded.

'I have bagpipes at my music studio,' Laurie revealed. He stopped playing.

Walter nudged Gaven. 'You could play the bagpipes to ring in the New Year. Having the laird play outside the castle would be a treat for the guests, and something to highlight on the website.'

'You're welcome to try playing them tomorrow to see if you've still got the knack,' Laurie offered.

Gaven barely hesitated. 'What are you doing now?' Gaven said to Laurie. 'Apart from playing the piano.'

'Just having a relaxing evening with the lads.' Laurie smiled over at them, thinking of their escapades in the snow and with the fireworks.

'Could I pick up the pipes this evening from your studio?' Gaven said to Laurie. The night was still young, at least in Gaven's world where late nights came with the running of the castle.

'Yes, no reason why not,' Laurie agreed and stood up.

'We'll take my car.' Gaven was eager to get going.

'Will someone tell Sylvia what I'm doing and see that she gets home safe?' said Laurie.

Sean nodded firmly. 'I'll drive Sylvia and Muira home after they've finished their crafting bee.'

Campbell and Ian nodded their assurance too.

Gaven headed out of the piano bar, followed by Laurie. He picked up his car keys from his office at reception, and put a warm jacket on while Laurie collected his jacket from the cloakroom.

The night was even icier than earlier as they walked out of the castle towards Gaven's car. It was sleek and expensive and could tackle the snowy terrain well.

Gaven glanced up at the sky. 'I think more snow is on the way tonight.'

Laurie agreed.

They got into the car and Gaven started up the engine and drove off. 'Thanks for going along with this, Laurie. Sorry to take you away from your relaxing evening.'

Laurie laughed. 'Walter will fill you in on that later. But in the meantime, tell me about your bagpipe playing.'

Gaven drove away from the castle, out the entrance and down the forest road. 'I learned to play the bagpipes when I was a boy, and played now and then when I grew up. I haven't played in years, so I'll be rusty. Maybe I won't be able to get a tune out of them. What about you?'

'The same as you. I can play, but it's been a while.'

Gaven continued down the forest road. 'Where exactly is your house?'

'Take the next turnoff just ahead. Follow the road as it narrows. The house isn't far.'

Gaven navigated the road well. The car headlamps highlighted the snowy terrain in their bright beams. There were no other vehicles nearby and the whole landscape had a quiet beauty to it, glistening in the night.

Laurie pointed ahead. 'That's the house over there.'

Gaven followed the road and parked outside the house. It was in darkness, but as they got out of the car, the whiteout created a glittering atmosphere all around them. Having accepted a lift earlier from

Campbell to Sean's house for dinner, Laurie's car was still parked there.

Laurie led the way to the entrance of the music recording studio.

Gaven was reasonably familiar with the property from years ago, but he hadn't seen it since the refurbishment.

Digging his keys from his jacket pocket, Laurie unlocked the door and flicked the entrance light on, illuminating the bagpipes on either side of the hallway.

'These look like new.' Gaven sounded surprised.

'They are. I bought them specially for the studio. It seemed appropriate to have bagpipes as a nod to the Scottish setting,' Laurie explained. 'I'm planning to play them on one of the new songs once I've finished writing them.'

Laurie lifted down one set of pipes and handed them to Gaven. Then he lifted the other set. 'They're different designs. The blowstick on your set is slightly longer, but they're both a good length.'

Gaven held his set. 'I like the longer blowstick. This set is similar to ones I used to play.'

'Come on through to the studio and give them a go.' Laurie led the way and switched the lights on, illuminating the hub of the studio.

'This is an impressive studio.' Gaven looked around at all the equipment and selection of instruments. Then he saw the baby grand piano. 'You've got a piano!'

'It just arrived. Don't tell Sylvia.'

'Ah, it's for her.' Gaven smiled.

Laurie looked slightly downcast.

'Something wrong?'

'I planned to show her the house and the studio once it was finished. And present her with the piano. I imagined I'd thought of everything. But tonight, when we had dinner at Sean's house, my plans got cast to the wind.' Laurie explained the details.

'I'm sorry,' said Gaven. 'Bad timing has scuppered me a few times when it comes to personal relationships. Especially when it comes to romance.' He sighed and shook his head. 'I'm single by circumstances, not by choice. I'd like to find the woman for me and settle down, but...'

'I know she's only going away for a season and then coming back, but it feels like I've missed my chance with her, that I should've organised things before Christmas. I tried, but the snow coming early slowed down the building work.'

'I'm obviously not the ideal man to be giving advice on romance, but if there's one thing I've learned it's speak up, tell her what you'd planned to do, don't pretend that you're okay with her leaving when clearly you're not.'

'In other words, open my heart to her,' said Laurie.

Gaven nodded. 'I've made mistakes in the past by keeping my feelings to myself. I'll never know how things would've worked out. But I see and hear all the gossip about local romances and I'm inclined to think it's better to tell her how you feel.'

Laurie agreed. 'Thanks for the advice.'

Putting this aside, Laurie let Gaven try playing the bagpipes.

Gaven was surprised how he took to playing them, remembering how he used to play. The sound resonated in the quietude of the studio.

'Well, now we know you haven't lost the knack of playing,' said Laurie, and then gave his bagpipes a go.

'Neither have you.'

'I suppose you'll be piping in the New Year at the ball,' Laurie surmised with a smile.

'Want to join me?' Gaven invited him.

Laurie hadn't expected to become involved, but liked the idea. 'Okay, we can practise here in the studio where no one will hear us.'

Agreeing to do this, they played again, together this time. The sound of the traditional song filled the studio.

'There's a wee room through the back if you want to try your dress on in private,' Jessy suggested to Sylvia.

'Thanks,' said Sylvia, keen to have a fitting with Penny.

Picking up her sewing kit that had her pins, scissors, thread and other items, Penny went with Sylvia and Jessy to make any minor adjustments needed to the evening dress.

Jessy left them to get on with the fitting, but when she came back into the function room, the ladies were talking about Sylvia's course.

'Sylvia's leaving in the new year!' Bee exclaimed while continuing to knit. 'I thought she was due to get engaged to Laurie.'

Muira nodded. 'We all thought he'd planned a Christmas proposal, but I think he got scuppered because his house wasn't finished. He probably wanted to make the whole proposal special and show her the house where they'd eventually settle down.'

The others agreed. Knowing that his house was almost complete, a few of them were working on finishing his housewarming gifts at the crafting bee night, including Rose. The appliqué cushion cover she was sewing was the second in a set of two she planned to give to him. The musical print fabric was from Aileen's quilt shop, and part of the same range of fabric they'd used to design the quilt they'd made for him.

Laurie's kitchen was due to be well kitted–out with hand–crafted tea cosies, tea towels, oven mitts, egg cosies and other lovely items.

Etta frowned. 'I didn't know that Sylvia wanted to own her own sweet shop.'

'She doesn't,' Muira was quick to clarify. 'The course was planned before she came to work with me.'

'It won't be of use to her now surely,' Jessy reasoned. 'What else will she learn on the course?'

Muira explained the details. 'But obviously her life has changed since she came to live here. Meeting Laurie is part of that. And now she's playing the piano again, something she excelled at before she gave it up to train in sweet making.'

'Sylvia is such a wonderful pianist,' said Etta.

'She didn't have enough confidence in her playing ability to aim for that as a career,' Muira explained. 'And she'd always enjoyed baking and making sweets, so that seemed like a more practical and attainable path to take for work.'

The ladies understood, but they were still unsure about her leaving.

'Is she set on going?' Aileen said to Muira.

'She hasn't decided yet,' Muira told her. 'I don't want to influence her or interfere.'

None of them did, though Etta was particularly concerned.

'It's bad timing if Laurie's house is nearly finished,' said Etta. 'He could be planning to propose. A New Year proposal instead of Christmas. Maybe he'll postpone the engagement again until Sylvia comes back in May.'

Muira agreed. 'It's such a key time in their romance.'

Etta nodded. 'I've seen other couples drift when they're apart. They go off to make new lives for themselves. The village is full of happy and successful romances this year, but I've lived here all my days, and I've seen plenty of heartbreak from couples making the wrong decisions.'

'The person Sylvia needs to talk to is Laurie,' said Bee. 'I used to travel a lot, always moving from one town, city or island to the other, never settled. When I came here for a short break to look after my aunt and uncle's cottage, I didn't think I'd stay. But now I feel like I belong for the first time, making new friends and joining the crafting bee. And I've met Campbell. Everything feels right now.'

Campbell hadn't proposed yet to Bee, but that's how their relationship was heading, especially as he'd refurbished the cottage as a potential home for the two of them. Bee felt the assurance of their romance and that they'd build a life together in the village.

'I hope Laurie handles it well.' Muira shook a shiver of doubt from her shoulders. 'I'm inclined to think from his reaction at dinner tonight that he'll encourage Sylvia to go. He won't want to be responsible for affecting her career.'

'What about Sylvia playing the piano on Laurie's new album?' said Jessy. 'Isn't she involved in working on the music with him?'

'She is,' Muira agreed. 'She made a fair bit of money from playing the piano along with him and his backing musicians. That's why she can easily afford to pay for the course and live in Glasgow.'

'I don't hear Laurie playing in the piano bar,' Etta noted.

Jessy checked the time. The crafting bee night was almost over. 'The lads will be finishing their hot chocolate. We'd better hide any gifts for Laurie so he doesn't see them.'

The ladies started to tidy away their crafts.

Sylvia and Penny came back in to join them.

'The dress is perfect,' Sylvia announced. 'It doesn't need any other alterations.' She smiled at Penny. 'Thank you so much. I love the dress.'

'Is that the one you'll be wearing to play the piano at the New Year ball?' said Bee.

Sylvia folded the dress carefully and tucked it beside her craft bag. 'Yes, I'm excited about it already. I'm playing in the piano bar. Laurie is going to sing and play his guitar here in the function room.'

Jessy told them about the bagpipe dilemma. 'Walter is hoping to sort out some music playing outside, but it won't be the same. Gaven is disappointed.'

As they were discussing this, Ian, Sean and Campbell walked in.

At first, the ladies didn't think anything of Laurie not being with them. They were eager to talk to Ian about the dance lesson.

'Is the foxtrot hold like the one we learned for the waltz?' said Bee.

'Campbell, come and help me show Bee the dance hold.' Ian beckoned him to come over and proceeded to instruct them.

The ladies were keen to watch and learn the proper hold.

Sean took Muira in his arms and danced her slowly on to the function room's dance floor.

'See how Sean's posture is creating such a wonderful top line,' Ian enthused to the ladies.

Muira giggled and enjoyed dancing with Sean.

Campbell followed their lead and danced away with Bee.

Ian smiled at Rose. 'Shall we?'

Rose smiled back at him, and they began to foxtrot around the dance floor. Rose tried to remember the steps and technique she'd learned.

'You're foxtrot is improving every time we dance,' Ian told Rose as they continued to dance around the room.

Walter came in, and seeing the couples dancing, offered his hand to Etta. 'Would you like to go for a whirl?'

Etta laughed and accepted Walter's offer.

Sylvia glanced at the doorway, wondering when Laurie would walk in so that she could dance with him. But there was no sign of him.

CHAPTER FIVE

Walter ran over to the sound system at the back of the function room and played the songs he'd lined up for Ian's class so that the impromptu dance night could have some music.

Apart from the crafting bee ladies and Ian and Walter, they were soon joined by Oliver, Fyn and Neil. They often turned up near the end of the bee evenings to pick up Robin, Aileen and Penny, sometimes staying to have supper at the castle.

Sylvia stood up from where she'd been sitting, anticipating that Laurie would be with Oliver, Fyn and Neil. She assumed he'd been waylaid chatting to them. But no, he wasn't there.

Seeing the dancing, Fyn was eager to partner up with his girlfriend, Aileen. Fyn was in his early thirties, tall and fit, with blond hair and blue eyes. He'd taken part in Ian's dance lessons before Christmas and wanted to learn more.

Neil had enjoyed learning to waltz for his wedding dance and took to the floor with his new wife, Penny. Ian's tuition had really improved his ability.

Oliver hadn't been a natural dancer when he participated in Ian's previous lessons, but he'd tried to learn how to waltz with his fiancé, Robin, so he joined in too. Robin's beautiful engagement ring had been designed and crafted by the goldsmith, Neil. Robin and Oliver hadn't yet set a date for their wedding, and were still in the throes of their recent engagement.

As the music and merriment filtered out of the function room, it attracted the interest of some of the castle's guests, and soon others started to join in. Most were couples and partnered up, but there were a handful of single guests. One of them, a fine looking man in his thirties, expensively dressed having dined in the restaurant, noticed Sylvia sitting on her own.

The man politely approached her. 'Would you like to dance?'

Sylvia's first instinct was to refuse, but then the man's warm smile made her change her mind, and she accepted his hand and walked on to the dance floor with him.

'People seem to be waltzing and learning the foxtrot,' the man said. 'Do you know the foxtrot?'

'No, only the waltz, but Ian's teaching the foxtrot here tomorrow afternoon, so if you're familiar with the steps, I'd like to learn.'

'I can foxtrot,' he said. 'I'm not an expert like Ian, but let's follow his lead and I'll teach you what I know.'

Sylvia danced with her new partner, while they both glanced over at Ian and Rose demonstrating the steps, the hold and the elegance of the moves.

But as she danced, even though Sylvia was naturally friendly and outgoing, and danced with other men at the ceilidhs, something felt wrong. In her heart, she was missing Laurie.

Noticing Sylvia apparently happily dancing with the guest, Walter didn't feel any urgency to tell her where Laurie was. Sean, Campbell and Ian felt the same. So everyone continued dancing, intending to tell her later. And thinking that Laurie could be back soon from the music studio.

Etta was now dancing with one of the guests. He'd invited her to try the foxtrot with him.

Walter partnered up with Jessy. As they followed Ian's instructions, Jessy noticed that she hadn't seen Gaven or Laurie for a while.

'Do you know where Gaven is?' Jessy said to Walter. 'And Laurie.'

'They're picking up a set of bagpipes from Laurie's music studio,' Walter explained.

'Bagpipes?' Jessy smiled. 'Does this mean that Gaven will be playing at New Year?'

Walter nodded. 'Hopefully. Gaven's not sure if he still has the blaw in him, but I think he'll remember how to play just fine. They left a while ago, so they should be back soon.'

Sean and Muira danced past Walter and Jessy. 'What a surprise, getting an extra dance lesson from Ian,' Muira called over to them.

Dancing on, Muira smiled up at Sean. 'It's a shame you were in the piano bar all evening. You missed a wonderful display of shooting stars in the night sky. We saw them from the function room and made wishes.'

Sean's smile was edged with mischief.

'What's that smile for?' Muira said to him.

'Nothing you need concern yourself about, Muira.' Sean swept her into the foxtrot and they continued dancing happily.

Laurie often surprised himself with how many sheets of music he had in his collection. Having dug through some of it, he'd found the music sheets for the three traditional songs they intended to play on their bagpipes.

Gaven stood in the music studio with the sheet music on a stand in front of him.

Laurie was standing opposite and had set the controls on the studio's equipment to record their session.

'Are you ready?' Laurie said to Gaven.

'As I'll ever be. I've never been recorded before, and certainly not in a studio like this,' Gaven admitted. He wasn't nervous, but a sense of excitement gripped him as they were about to begin.

'It always helps to hear yourself playing,' Laurie advised. 'Any bad habits or rough notes can be smoothed out after you've listened to your performance.'

The word performance jarred Gaven, reminding him of the responsibility to get this right. The chimes to ring in the New Year were such an integral part of the celebrations. Everyone would enjoy the buffet and dancing throughout the last evening of December. Then leading up to the last minutes of the year, the guests would get ready to countdown and cheer the beginning of January.

Laurie saw the flicker of tension in Gaven's face.

'You don't have to play this perfect first time,' Laurie told him. 'You just need to nail it in one.'

Gaven laughed, and this eased the tension instantly. He nodded to Laurie, knowing what he'd done and appreciating it.

'I'll give you a nod, then you begin,' said Laurie. 'I'll join in after a minute.'

'Okay,' Gaven confirmed.

Laurie activated the controls, then stood opposite Gaven, each with their bagpipes ready to play.

The seconds ticked by, and then Laurie gave Gaven the nod.

Gaven began playing on cue, reading the music on the stand in front of him, but knowing the song by heart, and ultimately playing more from memory, but the reminder of the finishing notes was handy.

Laurie joined in as agreed, and their playing circled the studio, resonating in the sound proofed confines of it, as no notes escaped and were captured clear and precise in the recording.

As the song reached a crescendo, Laurie and Gaven glanced at each other. No wrong notes so far. An impressive performance from them both.

Don't waste it now, Gaven urged himself, looking at the ending notes on the sheet music and nailing it to the last one.

The tone resonated for a moment after they'd both finished, the richness of the sounds lingering well.

Laurie signalled to Gaven to keep quiet for a few moments and then turned off the recording, capturing everything as planned.

'Well played,' Laurie said to Gaven.

Still holding their bagpipes, they gave each other a cheery high–five.

Laurie sat down at the control desk and prepared the playback. 'Let's listen to it.'

The song began with the single playing from Gaven and then when Laurie joined in, it sounded as if they'd rehearsed their performance.

'We'll practise again here in the studio tomorrow and any chance we get before Hogmanay,' said Laurie. 'We nailed it, but it's better to get some practise in.'

Gaven agreed. 'Let's do that. Thanks for your help, Laurie.'

'It'll be a performance to remember,' said Laurie.

'I've hired Gare to video the highlights of the New Year ball. I'll tell him we'll be playing outside.'

Gare was a local farmer and available to film events with his new video camera. Marginally younger than his brother, Fyn, he'd filmed various events at the castle in the past few months.

Laurie was about to switch the lights off in the studio when he noticed Gaven looking at the various instruments, including the guitars.

'Do you play any other instruments apart from the bagpipes?' said Laurie. He already knew that Gaven didn't play the piano.

'No, nothing. I never learned anything else. But if I had, it would've been the guitar.'

'Acoustic or electric?'

Gaven admitted a deep–seated longing. 'Electric.'

Laurie picked up a red electric guitar from a stand, plugged it in and played the opening riff to one of his songs.

Hearing it played live in the studio, Gaven thoroughly enjoyed it, but didn't expect Laurie to then hand it to him.

Gaven took charge of the electric guitar, putting the strap around his neck and holding it as he'd seen Laurie do it.

'Come on, give it a go,' Laurie encouraged him. 'You can obviously read music, and I think you play by ear as well.'

Gaven strummed his fingers on the strings, feeling the electric power of the notes resonate through him, and the charge of excitement that it brought with it. 'No wonder you love playing.'

Laurie gave him a quick lesson on how to play the guitar, and then picked up a black electric guitar and started playing one of his well–known songs. 'Join in, Gaven.'

Encouraged to try, Gaven started to strum, picking out the notes as best he could. Together their playing sounded great.

They were smiling and laughing as they played. Both their nights had gone from being downcast to uplifted by the joy of the music. And they played for longer than either of them intended, well into the night.

The impromptu dance lesson night in the function room continued longer than planned too, but guests were loving it, as were the crafting bee ladies and their partners.

Sylvia ended up dancing with another two men, and the evening became an unexpected success.

Chef had popped in to see what was going on, and to check if anyone required more tea or refreshments, and ended up being pulled into the dancing. At one point, the large dance floor was so busy that chef could only be distinguished by the kitchen staff that were looking for him, by his white hat in the middle of the happy melee.

Walter danced with Jessy. 'Gaven's not back yet.' He sounded concerned. 'I'm guessing that he's trying to relearn how to play the bagpipes.'

'Gaven tries his utmost as the castle's laird not to let anyone down,' said Jessy. 'But maybe you'll have to filter bagpipe music outside this year. We won't make Gaven feel bad. He's disappointed enough as it is.'

Walter nodded firmly.

'Does Laurie play the pipes?'

Walter shook his head. 'Ian mentioned this to him, but Laurie is the same as Gaven. He hasn't played in years. Besides, he's singing and performing his own songs and playing guitar at the ball. We can't expect him to play the bagpipes as well.'

'You're right,' said Jessy. 'We won't mention it.'

Ian and Rose danced over to Walter and Jessy.

'Walter!' Ian called to him. 'Can you play something snazzy and lively to finish the night?'

'Aye, I've got plenty of lively songs.' Walter hurried over and changed the music.

'I thought we'd finish with a slow, romantic waltz,' Rose said to Ian as they danced away.

'Nah, let's liven things up.' Ian's smile told her he was up to mischief. 'Fancy doing a samba?'

'No, Ian, I can't—' Rose's reply was drowned out by the lively music that kicked in.

Walter ran back over and rejoined Jessy. 'I don't know what Ian has planned, but are you up for it?'

Jessy laughed. 'Yes, why not. This is our last crafting bee night of the year. Let's celebrate it in style.'

Ian was showing Rose and others how to do the samba. 'Try some samba rolls, like this.' He clasped Rose from behind and began to demonstrate, causing Rose to giggle.

Seeing Ian demonstrate some of the moves, the bounce, the voltas and the rolls, everyone started to samba.

'It's all in the bounce action,' Ian called out over the music. 'Just let yourself go. Roll those hips.'

'This is the liveliest last dance I've had in a long time,' Muira said to Sean. 'And I didn't know you could do the samba.'

Sean pulled her close and did samba rolls with Muira. 'Oh, yes. Come on, Muira, go a wee bit wild tonight.'

Laughing, Muira and the other ladies from the crafting bee finished the evening abuzz with energy and fun.

Gaven blinked as he walked in and stood at the doorway of the function room. What had happened to the crafting bee night? He could see Ian demonstrating the samba with Rose. Numerous couples were joining in. And was that chef in the thick of it?

'You're just in time to join in the last dance,' Walter shouted over to Gaven.

'Oh, there's the laird,' one of the ladies, a guest, exclaimed, and ran over to him.

Gaven didn't resist being pulled into the samba by her, or giving it a go. It had been one of those evenings that he'd long remember. From playing the bagpipes and electric guitar, it was somehow fitting to finish with a lively samba.

Everyone from the guests to the crafting bee ladies were having a great time at the castle, and Gaven was happy to join in the dancing.

CHAPTER SIX

As the dancing finally finished, guests filtered out of the function room having enjoyed their evening.

Walter approached Gaven. 'Did you play the bagpipes at Laurie's studio?'

'Yes, and I'm going to play them at the New Year ball,' Gaven revealed.

Walter smiled. 'That's great.'

'I'm planning to go back to the studio in the morning to get some more practise in,' said Gaven.

Jessy overheard their conversation, and soon the news circulated around the crafting bee ladies and others. Everyone was delighted that Gaven was going to play the bagpipes.

'I left Laurie working away on his music and songwriting at the studio,' Gaven told Sylvia and Muira.

By now, they'd found out that Laurie and Gaven had gone to the studio, and Sylvia assumed Laurie would've headed back to his cabin.

'I'll let Laurie get on with writing his songs,' said Sylvia. It was late in the evening and she decided to go home, taking a lift from Sean.

Wrapping up in their coats and jackets against the freezing cold night, the ladies and others headed outside.

The colourful Christmas lights on the outdoor tree provided the only warmth amid the snowy landscape. The castle's gardens were iced white and merged into the trees where the cabins were dotted in niches within the vast estate. The long driveway from the castle to the entrance gates was covered with snow. A few solar lights had held on to the winter sunlight and shone along the edges.

Ian drove away from the castle with Rose.

'What a night!' Rose exclaimed.

'It was fun. From fireworks and sledging to foxtrot and samba,' said Ian.

Rose glanced at him. 'Fireworks and sledging?'

Ian laughed. 'I'll tell you about it some other time.' He changed the subject to the dancing. 'You seemed to enjoy dancing the samba. Many of the guests told me they want to learn the samba and foxtrot at the lesson.'

'Etta and the other ladies were right when they said that things don't quieten down here after Christmas.'

'It's going to be a lively night at the New Year ball,' said Ian.

Several cars, including Ian's, drove down the forest road from the castle.

Sean took Muira and Sylvia in his car, while Campbell drove Bee home.

'What are you plans for the dancing lesson tomorrow afternoon?' Sean said to Muira and Sylvia.

'We've decided to go to the lesson and the dance party at night,' Muira told him. 'We'll keep the shop open until lunchtime, and post off any online orders before we close.'

Sylvia had volunteered to tend the shop while Muira went to the lesson with Sean, but Muira insisted that they both go as it was the last lesson of the year.

Sean pulled up outside the sweet shop and Sylvia stepped out carrying her bag and the evening dress.

She waved to them as Sean drove away to take Muira home to her cottage.

Twinkle lights from the window display lit up the shop in a festive glow, and Sylvia went through to her bedroom at the back of the premises. She hung up the evening dress on the outside of the wardrobe. The sequins glittered in the nightglow shining through the window.

The dress was perfect for playing the piano at the castle for the New Year ball. But she hadn't decided what songs to include in her performance.

Getting ready for bed, she thought about several songs that would be suitable, and looked through the sheet music she kept in a small red vintage suitcase, picking out a selection to take with her to the castle the following afternoon. While she was there, she hoped to fit in a brief rehearsal. She didn't own a piano, so she relied on being able to practise her performances playing the one in the castle's piano bar.

And she thought about Laurie working on his songwriting in his new studio, wondering when he'd invite her to see the studio. Soon, she surmised, as it seemed to be nearly finished.

Feeling the tiredness wash over her, she went to bed and lay there gazing out at the night sky, hearing the classical tunes in her mind, and fell asleep to the harmonic melody of a beautiful rhapsody.

Laurie played his electric guitar in his studio, recording the melody, listening to the playback, and adjusting the chorus, making it more dynamic.

Jamming with Gaven seemed to have ignited his creativity and he put it to practical use by laying down the opening riff of a new song he'd been writing.

The lyrics felt like a whisper he couldn't quite get right. Maybe it was the revelation from Sylvia about the possibility of her leaving that had jarred his senses too, but any lyrics that sprang to mind had a melancholy element to them. This wasn't necessarily a bad thing. He needed a variety of songs on the album. One that tugged at the heartstrings could be popular and add balance to the otherwise upbeat selection.

Laurie had taken a creative break at the castle to help him write new songs, but now that he'd found happiness with Sylvia, his songs tended to be upbeat.

He played long and loud, secure that no one could hear him in the sound proofed studio. And in the seclusion of his new house, far enough away from the village main street and other properties so as not to disturb anyone. But near enough to be part of the community.

I have to let you go
Though it tears my heart in two
And hope you'll come back to me...

Laurie played around with the lyrics as the melody from his guitar filled the studio.

Gaven took his jacket and tie off and unbuttoned his shirt after bidding goodnight to the guests downstairs.

Despite the cold, he opened one of the windows in his turret and gazed out at the view. Amid the vast covering of snow, he could see the loch, the surface shining like glass, and the lights of the little main street twinkling beyond the loch. It was a view he enjoyed most evenings, and especially when he needed to unwind after a hectic day at the castle.

Playing the bagpipes at Laurie's studio had been a new experience, one he was still contemplating, along with trying his hand with the electric guitar.

He took a deep breath of the cold, fresh air, taking time to rethink the plans for the New Year ball. The poster didn't need changed. It had listed a piper playing the bagpipes but hadn't specifically named him. Now he was the piper, and Laurie had agreed to back him up.

Laurie was joining him for an early breakfast, then they were driving to the studio to practise playing the bagpipes. He'd probably forgo strumming the electric guitar, but no promises on that.

Laurie had offered to let him take the bagpipes away with him, but Gaven didn't want to play within earshot of the guests. So they were kept at the studio for the time being.

Gaven kept the window open as he stripped off and got ready for bed, filling the turret with fresh air, sensing the end of yet another great year at the castle. It was true that anyone imagining that things slowed down around here after Christmas were in for a lively surprise. And now that included him playing the bagpipes with a famous singer.

Laurie finally locked up the studio for the night and headed outside to his car.

The music was still playing in his thoughts as he drove away, navigating the narrow route that led to the forest road and into the castle's estate to his cabin. There was no one else around, and as he parked beside his cabin and stepped out into the snow, he gazed up at the vast night sky. Nearby, the castle was a magnificent silhouette against the dark sky and the snowscape. A soft glow shone from the entrance, lit with two old–fashioned lamps, but the front door was now shut against the night.

Laurie's breath circled around him as he dug his keys from the pocket of his jeans, clicked open the door and stepped inside.

Even in the depths of winter, the cabin never felt cold, and although he was looking forward to moving into his new house, he'd miss the cosy comfort of his little bolthole.

Nothing had changed since he'd left there earlier in the day to drive to the studio, and yet everything felt different.

Shrugging off his jacket, he started to get ready for bed. His bedroom window ran the length of the cosy room and in the summer had offered a view of the flowers outside his cabin. Then autumn gilded everything in shades of bronze and copper. Neither view outshone the other. The changing seasons in Scotland each brought their own beauty to the fore. Now the view was a glistening masterpiece of nature in the heart of winter.

Before getting into bed, he wandered through to the living room and reached up to the highest shelf where he kept a precious secret.

In his hand was a small velvet box. He opened it, and in the nightglow shining through the cabin windows, the diamond ring sparkled. Set in white gold, the three diamond design had been specially created by Neil the goldsmith. Laurie had commissioned the ring to be made before Christmas in the hope that the house would be finished by then. Since then, his plans had been adjusted rather than put on ice. But now...

His heart felt a deep longing to restore the hope he'd had before dinner when Sylvia had spoken about leaving. It was surely his imagination, but the ring didn't sparkle as bright now. Hopes dimmed, he closed the box and went to bed.

He checked his phone for messages before going to sleep. There was a missed message from Sylvia telling him that she was going to the dancing lesson and wondering if he'd be there.

Laurie replied:

I'll be there, Sylvia. Love, Laurie. x.

He waited to see if there was a reply, but it was late at night, so she was surely sound asleep, and would read his message in the morning.

Breakfast smelled delicious.

Laurie walked into the guests' dining room early the following morning to join Gaven at the laird's private table.

Gaven was already seated and had selected what he wanted from the menu.

'Chef's special,' Gaven said firmly.

'What's in it?' Laurie opened the menu and skimmed the items.

'What's not. Lorne sausage, tattie scones, eggs, grilled tomatoes, mushrooms, tea and toast.'

Laurie closed his menu. 'My type of breakfast for a busy day ahead.'

A member of staff took their order, leaving Gaven and Laurie to chat for a few minutes about their plans to play the bagpipes.

'We can take my car again unless you need yours to drive back here later,' said Gaven.

'I'm not lingering at the studio,' Laurie told him. 'I'm coming back for the dance lesson.' He'd had a cheery reply from Sylvia as he'd walked from his cabin to the castle for breakfast. She was happy that he'd be at the dance lesson.

'How's your foxtrot?' Gaven said as their breakfast was served up.

'I've no idea. I always think of the foxtrot as sort of a waltz, but not as fast as a quickstep.'

'Ian's determined to teach us the samba too.'

'We've chosen the right breakfast then,' said Laurie, tucking in.

Gaven nodded. 'We're going to need all the energy we can get. Remember, there's dancing later in the evening when we get to practise what we've learned from Ian.'

'That man has boundless energy,' Laurie mumbled, enjoying his breakfast.

Gaven smirked. 'From what I hear, you, Walter and a few other rascals had plenty of energy to enjoy a wild time sledging last night.'

'No secrets around here.'

'Nope.'

Perhaps one, Laurie thought to himself. The engagement ring he'd bought for Sylvia was a secret. Neil had assured him he wouldn't tell anyone.

After they'd finished breakfast, Gaven and Laurie went through to the reception where Gaven updated Walter on what his plans were for the morning.

While Gaven spoke to Walter, Sean walked through reception, having handed in a delivery of honey to chef in the castle's kitchen.

Sean smiled when he saw Laurie and they stood for a few moments near the doorway talking privately.

'I haven't had a chance to speak to you,' Sean said to Laurie. 'But I noticed you seemed concerned by Sylvia's comment at dinner last night.'

Laurie nodded. 'I didn't expect her to be leaving, or considering this. It threw me. I'm planning to talk to her later today, see what her plans are. But I've no intention of interfering with her career. Has she said anything to you or Muira about her decision?'

'No. I drove Sylvia home to the sweet shop last night, but she never mentioned about the course to Muira and me.' Sean glanced over to where Gaven was talking to Walter, and kept his voice down so as not to be overheard. 'I don't know what your plans are, but folk expected you'd be making a special announcement soon.'

Laurie sighed heavily and nodded. 'Gaven advised me to speak up, tell her what I'd planned and not pretend to be okay with her leaving.'

'That would be my advice too.'

Gaven came over to join them, and the conversation changed to the bagpipe playing as they all headed outside the castle.

'We're away to the music studio to practise playing the bagpipes,' Gaven said to Sean as they walked to their cars.

Sean looked surprised. 'Are both of you playing the bagpipes at New Year?'

'We are,' Gaven confirmed. 'Laurie has agreed to back me up.'

'What songs are you playing?' said Sean.

Laurie told him the traditional songs they were due to play. 'But I've looked out sheet music for another song that's less classic and a wee bit of a wildcard number.'

Gaven frowned. 'Does it involve playing the electric guitar again?'

Sean laughed. 'I didn't know you played the guitar, Gaven.'

'Neither did I until Laurie handed me one of the guitars he'd played on tour,' Gaven explained.

'Gaven can read music, and played the bagpipes well, so I thought I'd encourage him to try his hand at the guitar,' said Laurie.

'Will you be playing guitar and the bagpipes at the ball?' Sean said to Gaven.

'No, but I'd always wondered what it would be like to play an electric guitar,' said Gaven. 'It was an incredible feeling, but I'm sticking to the bagpipes and leaving the guitar playing to Laurie.'

Sean stopped beside his car. 'Well, enjoy your rehearsal this morning. No doubt I'll see the two of you at Ian's dance lesson this afternoon.'

'You will,' Gaven confirmed.

They got into their cars and drove off, heading away from the castle and down the forest road where Gaven took the turnoff for Laurie's studio, while Sean continued on down towards the loch.

In the bright morning sunlight the house and the surrounding garden and fields looked dazzling covered with snow.

'I'll be moving into the house soon,' Laurie told Gaven. 'The work is done and it's been decorated and furnished.' There was a wistful tone to Laurie's comment.

'You're booked into the cabin until the end of January,' Gaven reminded him. 'There's no hurry to leave. And as I've said before, you're welcome to go for a run in the estate as you've been doing while you're a guest.'

'I appreciate that. I love running through the estate, being outdoors.' He looked at the surrounding scenery. 'I'll be exploring this area too.'

They stepped out into the deep snow and walked towards the music studio. The air was so crisp and cold that nothing had melted even in the sunlight. Everything was frozen solid, creating an icy beauty all around them.

The two sets of bagpipes no longer hung on the walls of the hallway and were now in the hub of the studio waiting to be played.

Laurie switched the studio lights on, illuminating the equipment and instruments.

Gaven wandered over to the baby grand piano while Laurie set everything up. 'This is similar to the one in the piano bar.'

'It is. Sylvia likes the piano at the castle, so I wanted to buy one that I knew she enjoyed playing,' Laurie explained.

'When are you going to show her this piano?'

Laurie shrugged. 'I don't know yet. I'm going to talk to her later after the dancing.'

Sylvia cut the Scottish tablet she'd made into bite–size squares ready to be packed up for the day's orders. The main street glistened with snow, and the morning sunlight shone through the front window of the sweet shop, highlighting the jars of sweets on display.

Muira had put a spurt on and packed all the online orders while Sylvia made the rich Scottish tablet, fudge and treacle toffee in the kitchen. The shop was filled with the delicious scent of vanilla, chocolate and treacle.

'I've looked out a selection of sheet music to take with me to the castle this afternoon,' Sylvia said, refilling one of the jars with sweets.

'Are you going to practise playing the piano before or after the dance lesson?'

'I'd like to practise a couple of songs before the lesson, and then do the same afterwards.'

'Sean says he's coming to pick us up in plenty of time for the lesson. I've brought a tea dress with me, and the shoes I wear for the ceilidh dancing. I'll change here when it's time to get ready.' As Sylvia lived in the cottage part of the shop, they often dressed there when heading out to parties and events at the castle. 'What are you wearing?'

'A dress, like yours, a tea dress style. Nothing too long for learning to dance the foxtrot.'

'Sean can dance the foxtrot. He was showing me how to do the sway motion when he came in for a cup of tea after he dropped me off at my cottage last night.'

'Oooh!' Sylvia grinned.

'Don't be bad. We were just dancing in the living room while the kettle boiled.'

And then they laughed and continued to pack up the sweet orders.

CHAPTER SEVEN

Sean parked his car outside Bradoch's bakery in the main street and carried a delivery of honey inside. The aroma of fresh baked bread and cakes wafted towards him as he approached the counter where Bradoch was serving Fyn.

A tempting selection of cakes, scones and pastries were on display. There were a few tables near the front window where Bradoch served up morning and afternoon tea. The fire was lit and added a warm glow to the light cream decor and traditional styling.

A fine looking man in his thirties with dark hair and dark blue eyes, Bradoch had a cheerful manner and his bakery was a hub for local gossip.

Bradoch smiled at Sean. 'I hear I missed out on all the fun last night up at the castle.'

Fyn picked up the bag of rolls he'd bought, but hesitated to hear the gossip.

'It was a great night of lively dancing after the crafting bee,' Sean said to Bradoch.

The baker, dressed smartly in his whites, smiled knowingly. 'I was talking about the sledging outside in the snow. And the fireworks.'

Fyn couldn't contain his surprise. 'I was at the castle last night and I didn't see anyone sledging or fireworks.'

'It was before you arrived,' Sean told Fyn, summarising the sequence of events.

'I would've joined in,' said Fyn, sounding miffed that he'd missed out. 'Are you lot going sledging again?'

Sean put the delivery of honey through in the kitchen. 'I'm not sure. Walter was the one that encouraged us. You should ask him.'

'I will,' Fyn said firmly. 'I'll talk to him this afternoon.'

Bradoch bagged a loaf of bread. 'So you're going to Ian's dance class?'

Fyn nodded. 'Yes, I want to learn the foxtrot with Aileen. I'm closing my flower shop for a couple of hours this afternoon. Are you going?' Fyn said to Sean.

'I'm going with Muira and Sylvia,' Sean confirmed.

Bradoch sighed. 'I've no idea how to do the foxtrot, but I'm going to the dance at night regardless. I'll waltz my way around the floor. Hopefully, I'll meet a nice lassie to dance with.' A single man, he lived in hope of finding romance like others had in the village.

'Well, I'll see you two later,' said Fyn. 'And I'm certainly going to talk to Walter about sledging while we've got the snow.'

'Tell Walter I'll join in,' Bradoch added. 'I haven't gone sledging in years, but I used to enjoy it here during the winter.'

Fyn nodded and headed out of the bakery.

Sylvia put her coat on and picked up the two bags filled with the sweetie orders.

'I'll take these to the post office.' Sylvia put her knitted hat on. 'I won't be long.'

A few minutes after Sylvia left the sweet shop, Sean walked in with a delivery of honey. He put the jars down on the counter, and gave Muira a cuddle.

Muira giggled and snuggled into him.

Sean looked around. 'Where's Sylvia this morning?'

'She's away to the post office. We've packed up the orders early today so we can finish on time to close the shop and get dressed for the dance lesson.'

'Has Sylvia said anything about whether she's going away on the course?' said Sean.

Muira shook her head and looked concerned. 'No, not a word. She's been chatting about the music she's going to play on the piano, and about the dancing.'

'I thought she would've talked to you about leaving, or not.'

Muira shrugged. 'So did I. But not a peep. I was going to bring up the subject a couple of times, but then I didn't want to spoil the cheery mood in the shop, especially as the morning has flown in and we'll be getting ready for the dancing with Ian.'

'I had a word with Laurie this morning.' Sean explained the conversation. 'He says he's going to talk to her later.'

'Maybe it's better that they sort it out between the two of them first before I chat to her.'

Sean nodded, and then pulled Muira into his arms and pretended to dance the foxtrot with her. 'Do you remember the sway I showed you?'

Muira laughed. 'There's no room to dance in the shop.'

Sean dipped her playfully in his strong arms and gave her a gentle kiss.

'Rascal!' Muira scolded him playfully, loving every moment of it.

Ian had been up early to practise the foxtrot in his cottage. Rose came over to practise with him. They used the small dance floor in his living room, and Rose wore the ballroom shoes he'd gifted her.

'I can understand why the foxtrot is one of your favourite dances,' said Rose. 'It's tricky, but I'm starting to love it too.'

'Try the feather steps again,' Ian encouraged her.

Rose did as he suggested and they moved elegantly across the floor enjoying dancing the foxtrot together.

The music playing in the background suited the dance, and it was one of the songs he'd listed for the lesson.

'I like this song,' said Rose.

'It's perfect for the foxtrot, like a piece of musical theatre. Walter has all the songs lined up that I've requested, so we'll be dancing to this at the lesson. Guests and others attending the lesson should enjoy it.' He advised Rose on her technique. 'Remember the heel leads.'

Rose corrected her technique.

'That's it,' Ian bolstered her. 'And keep the flow smooth as if you're gliding across the dance floor.'

They continued practising the foxtrot and then Ian suggested they try the samba.

'You're really getting the hang of those voltas,' said Ian. 'Now let's do some samba rolls together.' Clasping her close to him, they did the rolls and then he showed her other steps that were part of the dance.

Bee was in Etta's cottage helping to make the housewarming gift package that the crafting bee ladies had made for Laurie. She'd walked over from the other side of the loch bringing the tea cosy she'd knitted.

Etta's cottage was one of several dotted around the picturesque loch. She often held knitting bee nights there. Her living room was homely and comfortable, and her stash of yarn was tidily piled up on the dresser shelves beside her sewing machine and the cutting table she used for her quilting. Knitting was her main interest, but she was a keen quilter.

'When Campbell told me that Laurie's house was finished, I thought we should give him the gifts,' said Bee.

'Sylvia says that Laurie is going to be at the dance lesson this afternoon,' said Etta, helping Bee fold the musical theme quilt the members had made for him. 'We'll give him the gifts then.'

Etta had been tucking the gifts into a large box as the members finished them. Rose's set of appliqué cushion covers and other items were added. It was now brimming with various quilted and knitted presents and other crafted gifts.

Bee and Etta put the quilt on top to keep all the smaller items, like tea cosies, oven mitts and egg cosies tucked in tidily.

The ladies had all signed a card for Laurie, and Etta put it on top of the quilt. 'There, that's everything. I think Laurie will be happy with his housewarming box. Fyn is giving Aileen and me a lift up to the castle this afternoon. We'll bring it with us.'

With their plan in motion, Bee had a cup of tea and a chat with Etta and then walked back across to her cottage.

The bright winter sky reflected off the surface of the loch and she enjoyed the crisp, fresh air as her boots pressed through the snow. The blues, whites and greys of the scenery reminded her of the latest colours of her new range of winter yarn.

Bee planned to spin more yarn before having a light lunch and then getting ready for the dance lesson. Campbell was coming to pick her up.

'I like the chanter on these bagpipes,' Gaven said to Laurie as they practised at the studio. 'The spacing suits me.' The chanter was the long reed part with holes that the piper used to play the notes. Gaven's fingers were placed ready for playing again. 'The sound quality is great.'

Laurie's set of bagpipes had a similar chanter, and he agreed with Gaven. 'Let's try the next song. I think you've nailed the first two.'

The sheets of music were set up on stands in front of them, and Laurie had recorded each song after they'd rehearsed it a few times. He'd then let Gaven hear the playback and anything they felt could be improved was worked on.

Gaven played on his own for two full renditions of each of the three songs, and then Laurie would accompany him. They played well together.

Laurie nodded, cueing Gaven in to play the third song that was part of their repertoire for piping in the New Year.

They began playing the song together, and then Laurie added a descant to their performance. Gaven kept playing but nodded, liking this version.

Laurie finally checked the time. 'I think we'd better head back to the castle. You've done exceptionally well this morning.'

'Thanks for giving me your time here in the studio. It's been great to practise without others, except yourself, hearing me try to get the tunes right.'

'You've clearly retained the techniques you learned years ago. The guests are in for a treat when they hear you playing. I'll cut a couple of the tracks and give them to you so you can put them up on the castle's website. I know Gare is filming the performance, but the sound quality is so much better here in the studio.'

'I'd appreciate that. I never thought of putting the bagpipe playing on the website, but I agree, I think guests and others will find it interesting.'

'The laird plays the bagpipes at the castle,' Laurie said as if it was announcement.

Gaven smiled. 'Accompanied by you.'

'Come back tomorrow morning for another rehearsal,' Laurie offered. 'We'll run through the songs again. It'll be our last chance to practise before you get busy with the New Year ball.'

'I'll do that, thanks. Join me again for breakfast.'

They agreed to this schedule, and then Laurie switched everything off in the studio and they headed out to Gaven's car.

Blinking against the bright glare from the snow and fierce blue sky, after having been in the confines of the windowless studio, they breathed in the fresh air.

Gaven looked around. 'It's a fine location to have your house and music studio.'

Laurie nodded and smiled, and then they got into the car and Gaven drove them to the castle.

'I'll see you later at Ian's dance lesson.' Laurie said, walking away to his cabin.

Gaven waved and headed inside the castle's reception.

Lunches were being served. Walter and Jessy greeted Gaven on arrival.

'Do you want lunch at your table?' Jessy said to Gaven.

'No, I've a few things to attend to, Jessy. I'll have something later from the afternoon buffet.' Smiling, Gaven went through to his office to get on with his work before the dance lesson.

Ian arrived with Rose at the castle. They put their coats in the cloakroom and changed into their dancing shoes. Rose wore a tea dress with a floral print, and Ian was impeccably dressed in a suit, white shirt and tie.

'Gaven is in the function room,' Jessy said to them. 'Away through. I'll be joining in the class later.'

'We're a bit early,' said Ian. 'But I wanted to make sure everything was set for the class.'

'It is,' Jessy assured him.

Smiling, Ian and Rose went through to the function room to find Gaven ensuring that the buffet tables were arranged properly on one side of the room. Staff were buzzing around, and Walter was busy sorting out the music on the sound system.

Gaven looked pleased to see Ian and Rose arrive.

'Everything's ready for you, Ian,' said Gaven. 'We'll work the afternoon lesson as we did before. Chef has planned the buffet for later on in the afternoon, but tea and refreshments will be served throughout the lesson.'

'Great.' Ian looked around. The function room looked festive and inviting, and he went over to talk to Walter about the music while Rose took a seat at the side of the dance floor.

A few minutes later, Jessy showed several guests through to the function room and introduced them to Ian.

Soon, others arrived, including Muira, Sylvia and Sean. Muira wore a wrap skirt with a nice flare and a blouse under her cardigan. Sylvia had put on a vintage tea dress, a bargain buy from Penny.

Campbell and Bee were there too.

Etta turned up with Aileen and Fyn. His brother, Gare, had arrived as well.

'Have you seen Laurie?' Etta said to Bee.

'No, not yet, but we're all slightly early. I think everyone's excited to take part in the lesson and enjoy the afternoon buffet.'

'Fyn drove Aileen and me here,' said Etta.

Fyn smiled. 'I've got Laurie's housewarming box in the back of my car. I'll bring it in later.'

Jessy overheard them. 'You're welcome to bring the box in and hide it in reception.'

'I'll do that.' Fyn hurried away, and Jessy went with him.

More guests arrived to take part in the lesson, and Ian was now in charge of the music system while Walter buzzed between the function room and reception.

Ian put on background music, and while Rose chatted to other ladies from the crafting bee, he circulated and met a few of the guests.

The lesson began on time, and Ian made a brief introduction, explaining the basic steps of the foxtrot and what they'd learn.

Sylvia kept looking at the door, wondering if Laurie was going to turn up, and was considering sending him a message when he came hurrying in.

'Sorry I'm late,' Laurie whispered to Sylvia. He'd become engrossed in his music writing.

'I'm just glad you're here for the dancing,' Sylvia whispered back to him.

'I've been teaching Rose to dance the foxtrot,' Ian announced. 'We're going to give you a short demonstration.'

Ian then danced around the floor with Rose while everyone watched them.

Afterwards, Ian taught them the basic steps and ballroom hold.

'Keep your posture upright,' Ian instructed them. 'It's important to keep your core strong. As you can see, Rose places her left hand lightly on my right shoulder on the upper part of my arm, and she clasps her right hand with my left hand. This is the hold we'll use for the foxtrot.'

Most of the guests had turned up as couples, but anyone without a dance partner was teamed up, and Walter and Gaven stepped in as dance partners too.

'Your frame is a key element of ballroom dancing,' said Ian. 'Don't lean forward. Keep your shoulders back, but down and relaxed. And remember to smile.'

Laurie took Sylvia in hold. It was the closest he'd been to her recently. 'You look lovely,' he murmured to her.

Sylvia smiled up at him.

Ian showed everyone how to do the feather step, natural turns and reverse turns.

'The slow foxtrot is a smooth, elegant dance,' Ian explained. 'The steps are longer as you can see when I'm dancing with Rose.'

Laurie began to foxtrot across the floor with Sylvia. He'd danced the waltz well during the previous lessons, and he danced well again, helping Sylvia to learn the steps.

Sean was able to dance the foxtrot and kept Muira right.

Campbell's style of foxtrot was similar to Sean's having learned to social dance from his father. Bee picked up the foxtrot steps dancing with Campbell.

Other couples, including Penny and Neil, Oliver and Robin, and Aileen and Fyn had fun dancing around, and as the afternoon progressed, so did their foxtrot skills.

During the lesson, Ian walked around, adjusting people's postures and holds, and danced with Rose.

After an hour of learning the foxtrot, Ian showed them the basic steps for the samba, again giving a brief demonstration with Rose.

'The samba is fun,' Ian announced. 'It has plenty of bounce action, samba rolls and other movements that I'll show you. Don't worry about making mistakes. Dance on, keep going, get back into the rhythm of the music.'

The samba created a lively atmosphere and everyone had fun dancing to the upbeat music and trying the samba moves.

Ian danced with various guests as well as Rose, and as the afternoon wore on, the buffet was served, bringing the lesson to a cheerful close.

'Well done everyone,' Ian announced. 'Remember, there's dancing here this evening, so come along and practise your foxtrot and samba.'

Gaven approached Ian. 'Great lesson, Ian. The guests really enjoyed the dancing.'

Laurie was about to talk to Sylvia before going over to the buffet. He wanted to invite her to his cabin so they could talk in private. But he didn't get a chance because Fyn walked in carrying the housewarming box, and he was surrounded by the crafting bee ladies as this was presented to him.

Taken aback, Laurie was genuinely delighted with the gifts and thanked the ladies for each one.

'These are wonderful gifts,' said Laurie. 'I appreciate you doing this, and I'll be putting them in my new house.'

As Laurie was swept up in the meleé of good wishes, Sylvia wondered when she'd see the house. But she pushed the thought of this aside, knowing that Laurie was busy working on writing his new songs. It was a hectic time of year for both of them.

Guests started to filter out of the function room after they'd enjoyed the buffet, and the crafting bee ladies and their partners headed out as well. Most intended going home to change and get ready for the party that evening.

Laurie thought he'd have a moment to talk to Sylvia.

'Would you like to come over to the cabin?' he said, holding the housewarming box of gifts. 'I'd like to talk to you. We haven't had a chance to—'

Before he could continue, Sylvia shook her head. 'I'm sorry, I can't. I have to practise the songs on the piano. I've brought my sheet music with me. And I've worn this dress so that I don't have to go home and change for the party later.'

Laurie felt his hopes sink further, but he nodded and smiled. He understood. He really did. Bad timing again.

'This will be the last chance I have to practise the songs in the piano bar,' Sylvia added. 'It's almost Hogmanay. Muira and I will be busy in the sweet shop on the last day of the year, and then we'll be getting ready for the ball. I don't have any other time available to fit in practising the songs I'm playing for New Year.'

'It's fine,' Laurie assured her. 'We'll chat some other time.'

Sylvia picked up her bag containing her sheet music. 'Yes, because I want to talk to you too.'

Laurie walked with her out of the function room to the doorway leading into the piano bar. On tiptoe, she gave him a kiss. 'I'll see you later tonight for the dance party.'

'It'll be fun.' He tried to hide the gnawing doubt that was tearing through his heart. It felt like things were conspiring to keep them apart. Under other circumstances, he would've invited her to play the new piano at his studio. But it was supposed to be a special surprise, part of his proposal plan. And realistically, it was the piano in the castle that she needed to practise on.

With a heavy heart, Laurie smiled and walked away carrying the box.

Sylvia lingered at the doorway to the piano bar, and called out to him. 'Laurie.'

He stopped and glanced round at her.

'I'm not going on the course.'

Laurie blinked. Had he heard right?

His expression made her clarify what she'd said. 'I've decided I don't need the course. And I don't want to leave.'

Laurie put the box down, rushed back to her and took her in his arms, gazing down at her. 'Are you sure?'

'Yes. That's what I wanted to talk to you about. I'll explain properly later.'

'I've felt turned inside out since you told me about the course,' he said. 'I would've waited for you to come home,' he said. 'But I wanted to tell you that I'd miss you so much.'

'I'm sorry. I didn't mean to cause you distress. I slept on my decision, and I realised something. For the past several years, I've taken one course after another — baking, patisserie, chocolate–making. I'm so used to going on courses. But now, I've found a great life here in the village. I'm happy. I'm enjoying working with Muira at the sweet shop. And I'm playing the piano again. I used to love my music, but I let it go to train in baking and sweet–making. Now I've found happiness here. And I've met you.'

Laurie pulled her closer. 'I love you,' he whispered, aware that some people were watching them, wondering if something was wrong. 'I'll see you later.'

Sylvia nodded, and then went into the piano bar to practise the songs.

CHAPTER EIGHT

I feel it's true
I've found the strongest love
The longest lasting love
Here with you...

Laurie bounded across the snow, carrying the box, heading back to his cabin, feeling like his world had become lighter again. The late afternoon sun created a burnished gold twilight, and as he unlocked the cabin door, he glanced over at the castle, seeing it highlighted against the sky. And he thought about Sylvia there, in the piano bar, playing the songs, and he was looking forward to dancing with her later at the party night.

Putting the box of gifts down, he didn't unpack it as he intended taking it to his new house the following morning.

His guitar was lying on the couch where he'd left it earlier to run over to the castle for the dance lesson. Lyrics were scribbled in his notebook. Poignant words that he was no longer in the mood to finish. He would, but not right now, as he was so excited that Sylvia wasn't leaving. Instead, he picked up the guitar and began working on a song he'd half–written days ago, feeling he could continue writing that one.

The words flowed easier with a romantic theme that matched how he felt. Writing the song, he thought about how to get his plan back on the right course. He had the ring, the house, the new piano. Now he needed the one thing he didn't have — time.

His proposal had been planned for that evening at his new house. Now they were going to the dance party, and he didn't have anything ready. He didn't want to throw a plan together for later that night.

Playing his guitar, he sang the lyrics he'd written previously, starting to hear the next lines spring to mind.

The piano bar was fairly quiet. Sylvia sat at the beautiful baby grand piano with her sheet music propped up in front of her. The classic piano was angled so that it faced outwards into the bar. It was under one of the chandeliers that showed the elegant dark finish on the piano, and suited the vintage design of the bar. Cocktails and canapés were often served there.

Sylvia had no qualms about performing a handful of songs to celebrate the New Year. Not from over–confidence, just a sense that she'd played from an early age for many years, and it was a part of her.

She'd selected sheet music for a rhapsody and a concerto, different from the ones she'd performed at the castle previously. And traditional songs from mainstream popularity suitable for the New Year ball. Previously, Walter had rigged up the sound system to pipe the music through from the piano bar to the function room. This was the plan again. Couples would be dancing to the songs she performed, and she imagined them waltzing and doing the slow foxtrot while she played.

Glancing out the window, she saw the golden glow of the fading light merge into a blue twilight above the trees around the edges of the estate. And a sense of excitement charged through her. So strong, she hit a wrong note, and had to correct her playing. As if she felt a change in circumstances, something wonderful in the planning.

Shrugging this feeling aside, she put it down to all the buzz from the dancing, the party that night, and the New Year ball almost there. Tomorrow was the last full day before Hogmanay. She knew she'd be busy at the sweet shop the following day. And then again on Hogmanay itself, the last day of the year. Walter's firework furore had been the source of what they'd thought were shooting stars. Everyone knew this gossip now. But she still wanted to hold on to her wish for romance that she'd made.

The romantic rhapsody she played resonated in the piano bar and the notes and sentiment drifted through to the function room that was being set up ready for the dance party.

Sylvia kept playing, practising a sonata, rhapsody and a concerto, along with a couple of traditional songs, and popular numbers, until the twilight darkened to a deep blue glittering with stars.

Laurie played his guitar by the glow of a lamp inside his cabin. Shadows outside the windows indicated that time had again slipped by him, but he'd finished the melody of the song's chorus.

Putting his guitar aside, he shrugged off any tension that had built up in his shoulders and then got showered and dressed in smart trousers, a shirt and waistcoat for the party.

His hair was still damp from the shower as he put his pale blue shirt on, leaving the top two buttons undone, but sharpening up his appearance with a midnight blue silk backed waistcoat.

Sylvia was playing the last few notes of a sonata when Laurie walked into the piano bar.

He stood beside the piano, smiling at her while she finished the song.

'That was beautiful,' he said, thinking how beautiful Sylvia was too.

The sound of guests mulling around in reception signalled to her that the party was gearing up.

'A few of the crafting bee ladies have arrived, along with Sean, Campbell and others,' said Laurie. 'Would you like to go through to the function room?'

Sylvia smiled, and folded her sheet music and tucked it in her bag. 'Yes, I'm in the mood for a party.'

'So am I,' Laurie agreed. He clasped her hand and led her through to find two vacant seats at the side of the dance floor. She hung her bag there, and looked around. The fire was roaring in the hearth, providing plenty of warmth to the large room, and two couples had already taken to the floor and were practising their foxtrot.

'I'll wait until there are more couples up,' said Sylvia. 'I'm not so confident about dancing the foxtrot, but I'm sure you'll keep me right. You impressed me with your waltzing at Christmas and now I find out you can foxtrot.'

'Only on a social level. Parties and functions have been part of my life since I was a boy, but I'm interested in the techniques that Ian's been showing us.'

'There's Ian now.' Sylvia looked over to see Ian arrive with Rose. She'd changed her dress from earlier into a lovely little cocktail–length dress. Many of the women had worn party dresses.

Muira, Aileen, Etta, Robin and others wore dresses they'd danced in at the castle's ceilidhs.

The ladies waved to each other.

'We'll let Sylvia and Laurie get a wee bit of time to themselves,' Muira confided to Sean.

'They both look happy,' said Sean. 'I'm guessing that they've figured things out between them.'

'It certainly looks that way,' Muira agreed.

Ian swept Rose on to the dance floor, encouraging others from the lesson to join in. Soon the floor was filling up with couples eager to waltz and foxtrot.

'Do you want to join in?' Laurie said to Sylvia.

She nodded and he led her on to the dance floor, took her in hold, and started to foxtrot with her.

The buffet tables had been reset with an array of dishes and refreshments. Staff unobtrusively placed cake stands filled with a selection of sandwiches, savoury pastries, pies and cakes. Salads and other dishes were added to the buffet menu.

Gaven peeked into the function room, and then went through to the kitchen to check that everything was running smoothly. He wore an elegant suit and the comfortable ballroom dance shoes Ian gifted him at Christmas.

There was rarely chaos in the castle kitchen. Chef was experienced in keeping everything on schedule, and Gaven expected to see chef in the thick of it, ensuring that the food was being cooked and served properly.

But tonight, when he walked in, Gaven was taken aback.

Chef, his white hat at a jaunty angle, was showing several members of the catering staff how to dance the samba, teaching them what he'd recently learned from Ian.

They were all so enthralled in their samba moves that they didn't notice Gaven had walked in and was standing near the doorway watching them. Totally entertained, he saw chef hitting a spoon off of a pot lid, keeping the samba beat, and relaying the count as he danced in the galley.

'And one, and two, and three,' said chef. 'Ian says the *and* is like a half beat between the beats.'

Gaven remembered Ian showing people how to do the samba voltas.

Chef continued. 'Ian emphasised that there has to be plenty of bounce and hip action in the voltas.'

The kitchen staff were giving it laldy, as was chef.

Gaven tried not to laugh, knowing they were about to see him any second now...

'Gaven!' Chef jolted to a halt. 'I didn't know you were there.' He put the spoon and pot lid down on the counter. 'We were just—'

'Practising your voltas and samba moves,' said Gaven.

'Aye, that's what we were doing,' chef admitted, fussing with his hat.

'I just wanted to check that everything is okay with the menu, the buffet, dinners for the guests,' Gaven said, prompting chef to nod.

'Everything is hunky–dory, Gaven. Nae hassle with the food tonight.'

'Fine, I'll let you get on with your...preparation.' Gaven then took them aback by doing samba moves out of the kitchen.

A roar of laughter erupted in the kitchen, and the sound followed Gaven out as he headed away, smiling to himself, and went back through to the function room to join in the party dancing.

After dancing the foxtrot twice, and then waltzing around the floor, Laurie and Sylvia took a break and went over to the buffet.

'The quiche looks delicious,' said Sylvia. It had tomatoes, peppers and courgette in the mix and she helped herself to a slice of it with a garnish of salad.

'I'll join you.' Laurie added a similar portion to his plate and poured two cups of tea. 'Do you want to sit down at our table?' He gestured to where they'd been sitting earlier.

Sylvia nodded and they carried their food over to the table and sat down.

She tucked into the quiche. 'I didn't realise I was so hungry. It's been a hectic few days. And tomorrow Muira and I are gearing up for a really busy day at the shop. Customers are stocking up on sweeties for their Hogmanay parties.'

Laurie ate his food and didn't interrupt as he listened to her schedule.

Sylvia took a sip of her tea. 'Then the day after that is the last day of the year. Hogmanay. And it's the New Year ball that night.' She changed the topic to his schedule. 'Are you all set for playing your guitar and singing at the ball?'

'I'm going to perform a few songs from my last two albums. Different songs from the ones I sang at Christmas. But I'm ready to play those.' He didn't mention about playing the bagpipes, something he was less confident about, but he planned to keep his promise to Gaven to back him up for the midnight celebration.

'Everyone's excited to hear Gaven playing the bagpipes.' Sylvia sounded enthusiastic.

'Gaven's coming to my studio again tomorrow morning for a final rehearsal. He's an excellent player. I've recorded him playing the pipes. I'm going to cut a demo of him playing so he can put it up on the castle's website.'

'Oh, great. I love the sound of the bagpipes playing especially at New Year. It's stirring and reminds me of the past. Jessy says he's playing outside the castle in the snow on the approach of midnight.'

'He is. It should be something special.' Although Laurie was playing back–up bagpipes, he wanted the spotlight to be on Gaven, stepping up and doing this to keep the castle's New Year tradition. 'And Walter is setting off the fireworks.'

Sylvia's face lit up with excitement. 'I love New Year celebrations.'

'You'll be part of them this year, playing the piano,' he reminded her.

'A Hogmanay to remember when we both perform at the party.'

Laurie smiled warmly at her, still wishing he could fit in some of his plans into her busy schedule. 'What are you doing tomorrow night?'

Sylvia's reply was instant. 'Muira and I have agreed to work late at the shop making loads of sweets, especially plenty of our Scottish tablet, my chocolate robins and other sweeties so that we don't run out on Hogmanay when there will be a last minute rush from customers. Then I plan to flop into my bed and get some sleep so that I've got enough energy to enjoy the ball the following night.'

Laurie nodded. This seemed like a sensible plan for an extra busy time for them at the shop. 'Then let's enjoy dancing tonight,' he suggested, finishing his food and drinking down his tea.

Sylvia's smile warmed his heart, and she got up, clasped his hand and they went back on to the floor to dance a romantic waltz.

'I didn't expect us to be dancing this evening,' she said as they waltzed around. 'But it's handy because we can practise in time for the ball. Penny altered a gorgeous yellow evening dress for me. I'm wearing that. It's got sequins on it. You'll see it on the night.'

Laurie didn't tell her he'd caught a glimpse of the dress when he'd been outside the function room with Walter and the others. Their escapade with the fireworks and sledging was no longer a secret. Local gossip had seen to that, but he didn't want to spoil her plans for the dress. And he hadn't yet seen her wearing it. 'I'm sure you'll look beautiful,' said Laurie.

Sylvia smiled up at him and they continued to waltz together.

The subject of his housewarming gifts came up. 'I'm taking the whole box to the new house rather than use any of them at the cabin.'

Laurie wanted to invite her to join him at his house the following day, but she'd be working, so he held off inviting her to view the new property.

'When things quieten down, I'd like you to see the house and the studio.'

Sylvia's face lit up. 'I'd love to.'

The music changed, and Ian encouraged everyone to try dancing the foxtrot.

Ian was partnered with Rose, and they demonstrated the steps, the smooth flow of the dance, adding feather steps and sways.

Couples enjoyed the dancing, the music and the whole party atmosphere of the evening.

'Are we going to do the samba, Ian?' Sean called out to him.

'Oh, yes!' Ian confirmed and gave Walter a nod.

Walter changed the music to an upbeat song and soon everyone was dancing the samba.

'Come on, Muira,' Sean said, encouraging her. 'Let's do some samba rolls.'

Muira kept laughing as Sean led her in the moves.

Campbell did the same with Bee.

'Remember your samba walks,' Ian called out, demonstrating the steps with Rose.

Laurie led Sylvia in the energetic samba moves, and as they danced past Sean and Muira, they smiled at each other.

There were some steps and movements that Sylvia wasn't sure about.

'I don't know how to do those!' Sylvia squealed and laughed.

'Hold on tight,' Laurie said, leading her in the moves.

The fun continued on the dance floor well into the night.

The dancing finally concluded with a slow romantic waltz.

Laurie held Sylvia close as they danced.

'I had a great night,' he said, gazing down at her.

Sylvia smiled. 'So did I.'

Laurie leaned down and kissed her gently as they finished the slow dance in each other's arms.

Everyone started to filter out of the function room. Guests went to their rooms or cabins, while others wrapped up warm and headed out to their cars.

Gaven stood in reception chatting to guests and waving people off. He was delighted with the party night and thanked Ian for encouraging people to participate in the dancing.

Laurie walked outside with Sylvia. She was getting a lift home with Sean and Muira.

Sean hurried with Muira to his car, opening the passenger door so she could get in out of the freezing night.

Nearby, Ian was driving off with Rose. Numerous cars started to drive away from the castle.

Laurie's breath filtered into the cold air as he kissed Sylvia goodnight. 'I'll see you at the ball.'

Sylvia smiled excitedly. 'I can hardly wait.' Wrapping her arms around him, she gave him a warm hug and then hurried over and got into the back of Sean's car.

Laurie stood there in the snowy night and waved them off, then he walked to his cabin.

Breathing in the frosty air, he gazed up at the vast sky arching over the castle and the estate. Thousands of stars glittered in the darkness. A new melody and lyrics started to filter through his thoughts.

Unlocking his cabin door, he went inside, turned a cosy lamp on and sat down at his keyboard. Hearing the music in his mind, he began to play the opening riff of the new song, and then the first verse, and the chorus...

As it was an early start in the morning, breakfast with Gaven at the castle and then the bagpipes rehearsal at the studio, he didn't plan to write too late into the night. But when inspiration like this struck him, he tended to write fast, as if the song was forged in the fire of his thoughts.

He recorded every note he played so that he could hone it later, and wrote the lyrics down. The words poured straight from his heart, edged with his feelings for Sylvia. There were times when he knew he'd written something special, and he sensed this as he played the notes on the keyboard.

The opening riff was always so important as it distinguished a song from the start. He stood up and went over to his electric guitar, switched it on and played the riff. The sound resonated in the night, and a shiver of excitement charged through him. This was the song he needed as part of his new album.

CHAPTER NINE

It had snowed again overnight, and Laurie breathed in the fresh early morning air as he loaded the housewarming box into the back of his car outside his cabin. He wore snug–fitting jeans with his boots and a sky blue cable knit jumper that Etta had knitted, and he'd thrown his warm jacket into the back seat.

Winter sunlight shone through the cold blue sky and glinted off the snow. The nearby castle looked picture postcard perfect against the beautiful backdrop of the surrounding forest and scenery. The second last day of the year was putting on a fine show, he thought.

Striding into the cabin, he picked up the notebook of lyrics, then locked the cabin, got into his car and drove the short distance to the castle.

He parked outside near Gaven's car. The plan was for them to have breakfast and then drive both their cars to the music studio. After the rehearsal, Gaven would head back to the castle while Laurie stayed to work in the studio for the rest of the day.

Gaven was talking to Walter at reception and they smiled when Laurie walked in. The laird wore his expensive training gear and boots, ready to tackle the snowy terrain.

'I've got a bag of fresh groceries for you,' Walter said to Laurie. 'Remember to pick it up after breakfast when you're leaving.'

'Cheers, Walter,' said Laurie, walking with Gaven through to have breakfast in the guests' dining room. Guests staying in the cabins could request fresh groceries to be delivered. He'd ordered the extra bag to take with him to the studio. The kitchen cupboards and freezer in his house were now filled with storecupboard groceries. Laurie had gradually stocked up in readiness to move in. But fresh milk for tea, and bread, butter, cheese and other items were handy to order from the castle.

Laurie sat down with Gaven at the private table for breakfast.

Gaven skimmed the menu. 'What are we having today?'

'Chef's special kept me going all day.'

Gaven closed the menu. 'It's going to be a busy day for both of us, so...'

Two chef's special breakfasts were ordered again.

They chatted while they tucked into their eggs, tomatoes, toast and tattie scones.

'I heard Sylvia practising the piano yesterday,' Gaven began. 'She's a wonderful player. Her song selection is perfect for the ball.' Then he glanced across at Laurie. 'The two of you seemed happy dancing last night. Can I assume she's decided not to go on the course?'

Laurie smiled and was pleased to tell him about her decision. 'I feel like a weight has been lifted off my shoulders.'

'When are you going to show her the new piano you've bought?'

'That's the tricky bit. I suppose I was cutting it neat with my previous plan, but...' Laurie shrugged. 'I'm making a new plan.'

119

'I hope I'm not taking up too much of your time at the studio.'

'Not at all. Sylvia is really busy at the sweet shop. I won't even see her today, so I'm planning to work on my songs. And rehearse the bagpipes with you.'

'I appreciate you helping me with this, Laurie.'

'It'll be a grand performance from the laird at his castle.' Laurie smiled as he ate his breakfast.

'You'll be backing me,' Gaven said, making sure of their plan.

'I will, but you take the lead.'

Gaven smiled, and then they ate their breakfast, drank down their tea and headed out to their cars.

Laurie put the bag of groceries in the boot, and drove off, following Gaven's car down the forest road. They took the turnoff down the narrow road leading to the house and studio and parked outside.

Gaven helped Laurie carry the groceries in while Laurie lugged the box of gifts.

Laurie switched the spotlights on in the studio and closed the door, effectively shutting out the world while they got on with their bagpipe rehearsal.

The delicious scent of vanilla and chocolate filled the sweet shop. Sylvia was through in the kitchen making another batch of nougat using the beemasters' honey while trays of the Scottish tablet were ready to be cut into squares.

The shop had been busy with customers popping in early to buy sweets for their New Year parties, and online orders were equally busy.

Ian peered in the window, looking at the jars of sweets.

'Here's Ian,' Muira called through to Sylvia as he opened the door.

'I'm in for a box of your special chocolates,' said Ian, breathing in the tempting aroma. 'They're for Rose to thank her for helping me demonstrate the dances.'

Muira lifted a box of the chocolates from a shelf and put them on the counter. 'Rose will appreciate that. This box has a nice selection of chocolates. I think she'll enjoy them.'

'They look perfect.'

Sylvia came through carrying a tray of chocolate truffles. 'Morning Ian. We loved the dancing last night.'

'It was a great night wasn't it,' Ian agreed, and hesitated when he saw the truffles. 'Does anyone ever come into the shop and buy only what they came in for? Or are they tempted to buy other treats?'

Sylvia and Muira smiled at each other.

'Do you want us to lie?' Muira said to him.

Ian laughed. 'Okay, in that case I'll have whatever those are.'

'They're chocolate truffles,' Sylvia told him. 'My own recipe. Some are rolled in chocolate sprinkles and others are dusted with a rich cocoa powder.' She held the tray out to him. 'We sell them in wee boxes so you can pick what type you want. There's white, milk and dark chocolate. Or I can make you a mix.'

'I'll take a mix,' said Ian, letting Sylvia select what he'd like.

'You'll like these,' said Sylvia. 'Customers are enjoying them. They're a new recipe.' She gave him one to try.

Ian popped it in his mouth and savoured it. 'Mmmm, thumbs up from me.'

Muira put his box of chocolates and truffles in a bag, and Ian paid for them, eyeing the chocolate robins and toffee frying pans while they rang up his order.

Ian sighed. 'And I'll have two chocolate robins and two toffee frying pans.'

Muira added these to his order.

Laughing, Ian left the sweet shop and waved to them as he walked away.

Next up on his to–do list was flowers. He continued along the main street to Fyn's flower shop.

The fragrance of the flowers wafted out as he opened the door and walked inside.

Fyn was working in the back of the shop, making bouquets and other orders. Peeking through, he saw Ian and smiled.

'I have to tell you, Aileen and I are loving your dance lessons.'

'I'm pleased to hear it,' Ian said brightly.

Fyn came through to serve him. 'What can I get for you?'

'Flowers for Rose.' Ian held up the bag. 'I have chocolates, but I want to give her a bouquet of nice flowers too.' He explained it was to thank her for helping him.

'You can't go wrong with roses, especially as they're her namesake.' Fyn gestured to vases of roses, white, cream, pink, red and deep burgundy.

'Perfect. Rose loves pink, and the cream are gorgeous as well.'

Fyn lifted one of each of the single stem roses in each colour and held them up to let Ian breathe in the fragrances. 'The perfume of the pink roses and cream roses is lovely.'

Ian agreed, and Fyn made up a bouquet of the pink and cream roses with greenery and tied them with a cream ribbon. Fyn added two Scottish thistles to Ian's order. 'For luck. All the best to you and Rose for the New Year.'

'Thank you, Fyn,' said Ian. 'We'll see you at the ball.'

Gaven played the final notes of the last song on the bagpipes. The sound resonated for a moment in the studio.

'You're ready to perform the songs,' Laurie told him.

Gaven nodded and put the bagpipes down. 'Again, I appreciate you taking the time to help me.'

'Glad I could help.' Laurie played the last recording. 'Listen to this. You nailed that last song.'

Listening to the recording, they both agreed that it was the best rendition Gaven had played.

'I'll cut that version into the demo,' Laurie promised him.

Smiling, Gaven got ready to leave the studio to head back to the castle and let Laurie get on with his songwriting.

'Take the bagpipes with you.' Laurie handed them to Gaven.

'I'll take care of them.'

'So you should.' Laurie grinned. 'They're yours now.'

Gaven frowned. 'But I—'

'I want you to have them,' Laurie cut–in before Gaven could object to the generosity of the gift. 'You'll probably be playing a wee bit more often at the castle once people hear you at New Year. You've been helpful to me while I've been staying at the cabin, and I'm going to be running at the estate, so...' Laurie nodded firmly. 'Keep them.'

Gaven was delighted with the gift. 'They're the best pipes I've ever played. The size, the tone, everything suits me. Thank–you, Laurie.'

As Gaven drove away, Laurie waved him off, then closed the studio door and began working on his songs, and his plans for Sylvia and romance...

'That's a fine set of bagpipes,' Walter remarked when Gaven walked into the castle's reception.

'Laurie gave them to me to keep,' said Gaven, showing Walter the quality of the pipes, and then he took them upstairs to his turret.

Gaven put the bagpipes on top of a dresser in the main room, and then got changed into his suit to get on with his busy day dealing with the guests and planning the forthcoming ball. Years of experience in celebrating Hogmanay at the castle ensured that everything was currently in hand. And now the bagpipe playing was his task to get right. He glanced at the bagpipes as he put on his suit, shirt and tie, hoping that he didn't need to practise again, especially here at the castle. Even from the seclusion of his turret, the distinctive sounds of the bagpipes would be heard by the guests and he didn't want to disturb them.

As he put his jacket on and adjusted his tie, he looked out the window at the snow–covered view, and saw the winter sunlight glint off the surface of the loch. More snow was forecast that night, followed by a freezing but calm evening for the New Year ball.

In the windowless studio, Laurie had no idea if it was snowing or not, and his priority was working on his new songs. He'd finished making the demo recording for Gaven and sent him a copy.

Sitting at the mixing desk, he listened to the chorus of his latest song, played on the keyboard and electric guitar.

Nodding to himself, he continued working on the opening riff until it sounded right, leading into the first verse of the song, followed by the chorus. The melody and rhythm worked well with the lyrics.

Taking a break from one song, he changed to a different track, listening to the music contrast with the previous piece. Creating an album was like putting the pieces of a musical jigsaw together, and ultimately he used his own experience, knowing how audiences reacted when he played live at concerts, to select the play list that made the final cut on the album.

Easing off the tension from his shoulders after playing for longer than he'd intended, Laurie went outside and breathed in the cold fresh air.

The scenery all around him looked beautifully dazzling in the remnants of the winter sunlight.

He took a picture of the house and studio in the snowscape, intending it as a treasured memory. But when he looked at it on his phone, he instantly thought it was a contender for the front cover of his new album. There was a timeless quality to the property set in the deep snow against the cold blue sky.

All his album covers were different, many his own designs or adapted from pictures he'd taken, or a still of him playing at a concert. The one thing that linked the covers was Laurie himself. He was always somewhere in view or the main feature of the design.

With this in mind, he walked over to a sturdy fence post and set up his phone on a timer, lining it up to capture him standing in front of the house and studio within the vast snowscape.

Taking several shots, he studied them on his phone and there was one in particular that looked like it would be perfect for the album. And fitting too, he thought, showing the new studio, the fresh start he'd made in the Scottish Highlands.

Happy with the pictures, he went back inside, made himself a cup of tea, and got on with this songwriting.

Ian had invited Rose over to his cottage for lunch. Wrapped up in her warm coat, she walked across the field, happy to accept his invitation. She'd been working on her quilting all morning.

When she went up to his door, she heard music playing, filtering out from the living room, so she stepped inside, took her boots and coat off in the hall, and called out to him.

'Ian, it's me.' She padded through to the living room.

Expecting to see him dancing, she frowned and looked around.

'I'm in the kitchen,' he said.

'Something smells tasty,' she commented.

Ian was standing at the cooker stirring a pot of Scotch broth. The kitchen table was set with two bowls, cutlery and a plate piled with fresh cut slices of bread from the loaf he'd bought that morning from Bradoch's bakery.

'It's nothing fancy, just broth and bread.'

'That's ideal.' Rose helped make the tea while Ian served up the broth.

He ran through to the living room, turned the music off, and then they sat together in the warmth of the kitchen having lunch.

Rose told him about the quilts she'd been making and he talked about the dancing lesson at the castle.

'I wanted to thank you for helping me demonstrate the foxtrot and the samba.' Ian glanced at the box of chocolates on the dresser.

'Chocolates!' She went to get up from the table.

'Not until you've finished your broth,' he said playfully.

Rose laughed.

They continued chatting about the dancing, and then Ian cleared their dishes away when they'd finished the broth and bread.

He lifted the box of chocolates and handed them to her.

'Oh, these are the special selection from the sweet shop,' she said.

She was so busy looking at the chocolates that she didn't notice Ian lift the bouquet of roses from the cupboard where he'd hidden them.

Rose gasped when she saw the beautiful bouquet. She breathed in the scent of the flowers and smiled at him.

'These are gorgeous. I love them.'

Ian put the roses aside for a moment and gently pulled her into his arms. 'And I love you.' He kissed her, and then helped her put the flowers in a vase of water.

For the remainder of the afternoon, Rose enjoyed dancing with Ian, having tea and chocolates, and practising the foxtrot.

The late afternoon deepened into an early twilight, and Ian invited Rose to stay for dinner.

She was happy to stay and they prepared dinner together, and it was times like this that she felt they were a long–standing couple instead of quite new. But she could see her future with Ian.

While dinner cooked in the oven, Rose set the table in the kitchen, and Ian went outside to the back garden and lit the fire pit.

After dinner, they sat outside, snuggled up in blankets, and sipped mugs of hot tea while enjoying the warmth and glow of the fire in the snowy night.

Rose gazed up at the stars, sparkling so clear in the freezing air. 'This is magical, Ian.'

Ian pulled her close and looked up. 'The night skies here are wonderful.'

Rose smiled and snuggled into him, enjoying relaxing outdoors on a winter's night.

Etta sat cosy in her cottage, enjoying an evening of knitting, and listening to her favourite show on the radio — the Mullcairn show.

Earlier in the year, Mullcairn had interviewed Laurie as a guest on the show in the studio in Edinburgh, and Etta and other ladies from the crafting bee, including Sylvia, had become part of the phone–in chat that night.

Since then, Mullcairn, a mature, strong, fine looking man, had become friends with Etta and the other ladies, but particularly friendly with Etta. A light but friendly flirtation had sparked between them, and he'd attended the Christmas ball where he danced with Etta and their friendship had deepened. Mullcairn had recently mentioned about the castle and Gaven on previous shows, so listeners were familiar with this.

Mullcairn's rich, presenter's voice sounded over the radio.

'To conclude tonight's show, I'm going to play one of Laurie's popular songs from a past album. It seems fitting to close the show with Laurie, as I'm heading to Gaven's castle tomorrow for the New Year ball where Laurie is performing. I'll report all about it when I come back to Edinburgh for my next show on the first evening of January.'

Etta stopped knitting and listened, keen to hear that Mullcairn was turning up to the ball. He'd told her at Christmas that he wasn't sure if he could fit it into his busy schedule in Edinburgh.

'*If you're listening, Etta, save a few dances for me at the ball.*'

Etta's heart beat excitedly.

'*And I've heard a wee bit of gossip that Gaven, the castle's laird, is playing the bagpipes to ring in the New Year.*' Mullcairn laughed. '*Cheers, for the news, Walter.*'

Etta scrambled to pick up her phone and sent a message to some of the crafting bee ladies, and Walter, alerting them about Mullcairn's message on the show.

Walter was the first to respond:

Aye, Etta, I told Gaven I'd tell Mullcairn he's playing the bagpipes. Mullcairn's booked into the castle for an overnight stay after the ball.

Mullcairn's voice sounded over the radio.

'*I'm going to play a few wee jingles and then conclude with a song from Laurie. Goodnight, folks, and remember to join me for the show in the New Year.*'

Etta picked up the jumper she was knitting and listened to Laurie's popular song as the radio show came to a close, excited to know that she'd be dancing with Mullcairn at the ball.

Sylvia turned the main lights off in the sweet shop. Muira had just gone home to her cottage. They'd worked all day in the shop, and into the evening, making sweets for the last minute rush the following day.

The twinkle lights in the front window gave a festive glow to the shop, and Sylvia took a few moments to gaze out at the main street, so quiet after the busy day, and covered in snow that gave it a stillness and beauty.

The next day was going to be hectic, so she got ready for bed, and snuggled under the quilt. Lying there, she thought about Laurie, wondering how he was getting on with his songwriting. And was looking forward to seeing his new house and music studio. But first, there was the busy day at the shop to tackle in the morning, she reminded herself, and then she'd put on her evening dress for the ball that night.

Watching the stars twinkle, she went over the songs she intended playing, thinking of the music, the melody of each song. And fell sound asleep.

Laurie drove away from the music studio late at night. His headlights illuminated the snow–covered road leading up to the castle.

He'd had a productive day at the studio, working on the new melodies and lyrics, playing the keyboard and guitars. And the baby grand piano that he'd had tuned on its arrival at the studio. The tone of it sounded wonderful, and he was hopeful that Sylvia would like it.

Driving up to his cabin, he parked beside it and stepped out into the freezing cold night air. Glancing over at the nearby castle, he saw that a few lights still glowed from the windows, but he appeared to be the last person up and about. As it was after midnight, it was now Hogmanay. He'd dance with Sylvia at the New Year ball in the evening, and felt excited about the dancing, music and celebrations.

Heading inside, he went to bed to get some sleep before the busy day began, and fell asleep going over the plans he had for the New Year ball.

CHAPTER TEN

Snow had fallen lightly overnight and the village main street looked lovely in the early morning glow of the winter sun. The air was cold and calm, but the shops were buzzing with activity.

Christmastime in the village was filled with festive fun and the twinkle lights on the large Christmas tree in the main street were switched on. But Hogmanay was celebrated with gusto. The last day of the old year was going out in a blaze of cheers and roaring into the New Year.

All the shops were open, their windows lit up, and busy with customers buying groceries, sweets and gifts for friends and family for Hogmanay.

There was already a queue in Bradoch's bakery with customers eager to pick up their orders of fresh bread, scones, fruitcakes, and his special New Year savoury pies rich with gravy and topped with puff pastry. And his popular all–butter shortbread.

Delivery vans hurried to unload grocery items and other supplies to the shops — everything from milk and cream to haggis, neeps and tatties. A load of turnips and potatoes were always needed at this time of year, and the wee shop where people bought their groceries had loads on display at the front of their shop. There were tatties for roasting, boiling and mashing. Beside the turnips were carrots, cabbage, onions, Brussels sprouts and parsnips.

Sean had stocked up again on fresh groceries for the New Year and put the shopping bags in the boot of his car. He waved to Muira through the window of the sweet shop, and popped in to see her.

Muira and Sylvia were busy packing up a large order of sweets for chef at the castle. Chef had ordered their nougat, truffles and various other sweets that he planned to add to the buffet that evening. He'd thought he'd ordered plenty in advance, but with the extra dance afternoons and evening parties having included buffets, his supplies were running low. But Muira and Sylvia had told him they could cope with the short notice order, and had spent the early morning preparing it for chef. He'd bought their entire supply of treacle toffee, butterscotch and macaroon bars.

Many of the local shops were closing at midday or early afternoon so the owners could prepare for Hogmanay. But the sweet shop was open until four o'clock to meet customers' demand for the tasty sweets.

'Is there anything I can do to help?' Sean offered, seeing how busy they were.

Muira took him up on his offer. 'Could you take chef's order up to the castle?'

'Yes, I'm delivering more jars of honey to chef, so I'll take your sweets as well,' said Sean.

'I was going to drive up with the order,' Sylvia explained to Sean. 'But it would be so helpful if you could do that, thanks.' To save time, she'd showered and washed her hair at the crack of dawn so that later all she had to do was brush it through, refresh her makeup and put her evening dress on for the ball. While she worked in the shop, she mentally rehearsed the songs she was due to play at the castle.

'It's all go this morning,' said Muira, packing up the bags of nougat, Scottish tablet and chocolate truffles. 'But it's always hectic at Hogmanay. I'll be glad to relax at the ball.'

Sean laughed. 'Dancing the night away with me.'

Muira smiled. 'Are you wearing your kilt?'

'I am. I've got it looked out and ready to put on later,' Sean confirmed. 'From talking to the other lads I think most of the men will be kilted. Campbell is certainly wearing his kilt.'

Sylvia filled a chocolate box with champagne and whisky truffles and put it in the window display. 'I'm assuming Laurie will wear his kilt, but we've both been so busy that I haven't had a chance to have a proper chat with him.'

'Things will slow down in the new year,' said Sean.

Muira looked doubtful. 'A wee bit, but Jessy says that Gaven has big plans for the new year.'

'It's probably to do with the new cabins that Campbell's been working on,' Sean reasoned. The cabins were a recent addition to the castle's guest facilities. Cabins such as the one Laurie was staying in had proved to be popular for creative breaks, and due to the success of these, Gaven had decided to have extra cabins built in niches around the estate.

Sylvia served two customers while Muira and Sean continued chatting.

'That's part of it,' Muira agreed. 'Though Jessy told me that Gaven has other plans in mind. We're thinking it'll be more party nights or events at the castle. So we've lots more fun to look forward to.'

'That sounds great to me.' Sean beamed a broad smile at Muira, and refrained from lifting her up as he often did in the shop and giving her a cuddle. With more customers coming into the shop, he didn't want to embarrass her, and there was barely room now.

'I'll come back in a wee while,' Sean whispered to Muira. 'I've fresh bread and other things to buy from Bradoch's bakery.'

Muira nodded. 'Thanks, we'll have finished packing chef's order by then.'

One of the customers was Oliver. 'I came in for a large bag of your assorted selection of sweeties. But I noticed your champagne and whisky truffles in the window, so I'll take a box of those too.'

Sylvia lifted a box of truffles from the shelf behind the counter, leaving the one in the window on display, and added it to Oliver's assorted sweets order.

'You're fair busy today,' Oliver remarked as he paid for the sweets.

'Yes, and we're open until four this afternoon. What about yourself? Are you keeping your art shop open all day?' said Sylvia.

'No, I'm closing at lunch, but I'll be upstairs working on my book illustrations making the time go in until I pick Robin up for the ball.' Oliver lifted his order. 'I'll see you later. I'm looking forward to hearing you play the piano again.'

Sylvia smiled and waved him off and then attended to the next customer.

Laurie stepped out of his cabin and went for a run in the snow, taking a different route from the last time.

Dressed in his running gear, he headed in the opposite direction, taking a route that led into the depths of the forest where the ground was thick with withered leaves, gnarled roots and barely any snow.

Shielded by the overhanging canopy of the intertwined branches of evergreens, the undergrowth looked more autumnal than winter.

Sunlight dimmed to umber shadows and he loved the atmosphere, the scent of the greenery and the shades of ochre in the heart of it. There was a calmness to the forest, which was just what he needed as he knew that New Year's Eve at the castle was going to be hectic.

The thickness of the trees in this part of the estate slowed his brisk pace, but he was curious to see if this route led to a clearing where he could see his house in the distance.

Emerging from the forest, there in front of him was a vast view of open fields. In the distance he could see his house set in one of the fields. He'd always been meaning to check whether he could run from his house, along part of the narrow road and into the forest from this direction. Once he moved from the cabin, he intended taking Gaven up on his offer to continue his runs through the castle's estate. This felt like it was still on his doorstep even though it was a fair run.

Laurie stood there for a few moments, gazing at the house, mulling over his plans. His breath filtered up into the bright blue sky, though there was nothing summery about it. The winter blue was dazzling and reminded him of the photos he'd taken outside his house and studio recently. On reflection, he was sure that one of the pictures would become the cover of his new album.

A deep longing to be with Sylvia shot through him, and he sent her a brief message:

I'm looking forward to seeing you tonight at the castle. Love, Laurie.

Turning around, he backtracked to where he'd come from and ran all the way to his cabin while the final words of a song's lyrics filtered through his mind.

Inside the cabin, he picked up his guitar and started playing the melody and singing the new song.

Sylvia dug into the pocket of her apron after she'd served several customers and checked the message on her phone from Laurie. She read it eagerly, and replied:

Love you too. Are you wearing your kilt?

Laurie saw the message from Sylvia. He put his guitar aside for a moment and responded:

Kilt, sporran and finery.

Sylvia smiled as she read his reply, and then got on with her work.

Sean delivered the sweets and jars of honey to the castle, carrying the items through to chef in the kitchen.

The kitchen was a whir of activity as food was being prepared for the lunches and dinners, and the buffet for the ball. Chef planned the lavish buffet to offer hot and cold dishes. Haggis was always a top dish, served with neeps and tatties. Along with the mashed turnip and potatoes, a variety of vegetables were available. Crisp salads and salmon dishes were on the menu, and pasta and quiche. Chef's traditional savoury pie with a thick layer of puff pastry was a key item on the menu.

Chef had made the black bun himself. It was a fruitcake rich with dried fruits and spices and encased in pastry. He'd made a few, and later these would be sliced and served on the buffet tables along with various other cakes and sweets.

Clootie dumplings made with flour, dried fruits, cinnamon, ginger and other ingredients, were boiling away nicely in large pans of water, ready to be sliced and served up with custard or cream as part of the buffet.

Huge soup pots were bubbling with Scotch broth and the delicious aroma made Sean decide what he'd have for his lunch later at home.

'The sweeties from Muira and Sylvia are in the bags,' Sean called over to chef. He put them down on a counter at the side of the kitchen. 'And I brought more honey.'

'Thanks, Sean,' chef called over to him while he decorated a large Dundee cake with almonds in preparation for the celebrations.

Sean headed away, but as he walked through reception, Walter waved him over.

'Gaven wants me to organise sledging for the guests after New Year,' Walter explained. 'Probably one day and an evening event. He's happy for you and several of the other lads to join in. Do you want me to put you and Campbell's names down on the list of participants?'

Sean nodded firmly. 'Yes, I'd love another go at the sledging, and I'm sure Campbell would as well.'

Walter added their names to the list. 'I'll phone the other lads or talk to them when they come to the ball tonight.'

'Chef seems to be putting on a lavish spread for us this evening,' Sean remarked.

'Oh, yes. Lavish is the right word. The Christmas buffet is always wonderful, but chef goes all out for New Year.' Walter glanced over to the function room where staff were buzzing around preparing the tables and setting things up. 'The ball starts at seven–thirty, and begins with ceilidh dancing. Then ballroom dances will be included. I've got a great playlist of music. And guests can help themselves to the buffet all evening.'

'I can feel the excitement building in the castle already,' Sean commented.

'I think it's going to be a really special night,' said Walter. 'And regarding the sledging, if Muira, Sylvia and Bee want to join in, let me know.'

'I'll tell the lassies,' said Sean.

Etta went into Aileen's quilt shop, tempted by the bargain bundles of pre–cut fabric in the window. Etta had been out picking up last minute grocery items and had seen the display when she'd walked by.

Two other customers were in the shop, browsing and buying.

Aileen was hurriedly bagging up fabric scraps from the off–cuts she'd kept, and smiled when Etta walked in.

'You've got your sale on early,' Etta remarked to Aileen. 'It's usually in the new year when you reopen after Hogmanay.'

'I'm still having my New Year sale, but I thought I'd tidy up the shop and put the bargain bundles in the display. Folk have been snapping them up,' said Aileen.

'I'll take the one with lots of ditsy florals and bright solids.' Etta pointed to the one she wanted.

Aileen lifted it out of the window and put it on the counter.

By now, Etta was eyeing the scrap bags of quilting weight cotton. 'Give me one of the scrap bags. They're so handy for quilting and other wee projects.'

Aileen picked one that was filled with a variety of colours and prints. 'I put one aside for Rose. She says it's great for her appliqué and quilting.'

Etta was happy with what she'd bought, and chatted for a moment. 'I've got my cottage all tidy for Hogmanay. I hoovered, and dusted the stoor from the nooks and crannies, and my washing was already done. So that's me all ready to go into the new year with a tidy wee hoose.'

It was traditional to clean your house to start the new year with a tidy abode for a fresh start, clearing away the old year and welcoming in the new.

'That's why I was tidying up the shop,' said Aileen. 'I like to clean the shop and have everything tidy for Hogmanay.' Aileen lived in accommodation that was part of the shop, and considered one to be an extension of the other.

Etta picked up her fabric that Aileen had put into a bag so she could carry it with her groceries back to her cottage.

'Fyn is picking me up tonight for the ball and we'll come and get you too as agreed,' Aileen reminded Etta.

'I'll be ready.' Etta smiled and headed out. She intended relaxing for the rest of the day, maybe even having a wee nap in the afternoon, so she'd be able to enjoy the long night of fun and dancing.

Campbell and Sean sat in the farmhouse kitchen having a bowl of Scotch broth and bread for lunch.

Sean told Campbell about the sledging.

'I'm up for another go at the sledging.' Campbell sounded eager. 'When is it?'

'Walter says it'll be a few days after the ball, while there's still plenty of snow. A daytime event and one in the evening. He's put our names down for both.'

Campbell smiled broadly.

'And he says Muira, Sylvia and Bee are welcome to join in. I'm going to talk to Muira later.'

'I'll tell Bee.'

'Sledging?' Ian said when Walter phoned him. 'Put my name down. And Rose's name.'

Ian was practising dancing with Rose in his living room, getting ready for the ball.

Rose waved her arms and shook her head at Ian. 'No,' she hissed at him.

'Yes, she's waving with enthusiasm, Walter,' said Ian. 'Okay, we'll see you tonight.'

Rose sighed at Ian. 'I'm not whizzing down the slopes on a sledge. I'll stand at the side and watch, maybe throw snowballs at you as you go by.'

Ian pulled her close and smiled. 'Fine, but you might change your mind once you see how much fun it is.' He compared it to the dancing. 'Look how you were reluctant to learn the foxtrot and the samba, and now you're enjoying dancing them with me.'

Music played in the background, and they continued to dance again, practising the foxtrot, and then stopped to have lunch together in the kitchen.

While they prepared a light meal, Ian chatted about other dances they'd practise after lunch. 'We should practise natural and reverse turns for our waltz.'

'You do realise that the New Year ball isn't the same as the Christmas ball,' Rose told him. 'There's dancing until midnight, then everyone celebrates the bells at New Year. But later, the dancing notches up a gear and continues well into the early hours of the morning.'

Ian's expression showed he hadn't considered this.

'The crafting bee ladies advised me to have a relaxing day if I could,' said Rose. 'It's going to be a long night at the castle.'

'Okay, after lunch, we'll snuggle up on the couch and watch a film. How does that sound?'

Rose smiled at Ian and gave him a kiss.

Walter added Ian's name to the sledging list. 'Ian wants to take part in the sledge events,' he said to Gaven as they stood at the reception desk with Jessy.

Staff were scurrying back and forth, preparing the castle for the ball. Gaven was overseeing everything. He'd done this for so many years, and things tended mainly to go smoothly with only a few hiccups.

Gaven had his own list of things needing done and had ticked off half of them. But an important task still required his attention. He looked thoughtful and then made his choice for the castle's first footing tradition.

It was a Scottish tradition to have a first footer. The first person to enter someone's home after midnight at New Year was thought to bring good luck. It marked the end of the old year and the start of the new one.

Often the first footer was a tall man with dark hair, and Gaven had someone in mind that fitted the bill perfectly.

'I'm going to invite Ian to be the castle's first footer this year,' Gaven said to Walter and Jessy. 'Ian ticks all the boxes, and he's done a lot to help with teaching the dancing and encouraging others to join in.'

'Excellent choice,' said Jessy.

'Ian is perfect as our first footer this year,' Walter agreed.

'I'll tell him when he arrives tonight for the ball,' said Gaven, ticking another task from his list. No one had yet refused to take on this special task and Gaven was sure that Ian would be happy to do this as part of the castle's tradition.

CHAPTER ELEVEN

Winter sunlight gave way to the twilight as Laurie walked from his cabin to the castle carrying two guitars and the bagpipes. The instruments were in individual protective cases and he'd tucked sheet music in with one of the guitars.

It was an hour until the start of the New Year ball, and he wanted to store the instruments before the festivities began so as not to make a parade of himself when he arrived later. He wore warm casuals as he trudged through the snow.

Lanterns and other lights had been added to the front of the castle to illuminate the exterior. The castle always put on an impressive display to light up the old year and welcome a bright new one.

Lights glowed from the castle windows, including Gaven's turret, and the front entrance door was open in welcoming.

Laurie carried the instruments into reception. Walter was already kilted, and Jessy was wearing her evening dress and attending to guests.

Walter saw Laurie and called over to him. 'You can put your instruments in the wee room you used at Christmas.'

'Thanks, Walter,' said Laurie, and hurried through reception and into the room where he'd kept his guitars for the previous performance. He put them down and headed back out, wasting no time as he wanted to get back to his cabin to get changed into his kilt. Sylvia had messaged him that she was arriving with Sean and Muira and would meet him at the start of the ball. He didn't want to be late.

Giving Walter an acknowledging nod that the instruments were stored safely, Laurie headed out into the cold again. Even in those few minutes, the twilight had deepened a few shades to an ultramarine sky where stars were beginning to shine. Luckily, it was a dry, still night, bitterly cold, but the crispness in the air would surely emphasise the enigmatic sound of the bagpipes playing at midnight.

Feeling a charge of excitement for the evening ahead, Laurie strode back to his cabin.

Gaven hurried down the spiral staircase of his turret carrying the bagpipes. He wore his dress kilt with his kilt jacket, waistcoat, shirt and tie, and looked immaculate. A skean dhu was tucked into his right sock with only the ornate silver handle of the small dagger visible. Part of the traditional Highland dress, he wore it on his dominant side, and had tartan flashes that matched his kilt tucked into the top folds of his thick woollen socks, worn with ghillie brogues.

Reception was bustling with activity, and staff were going back and forth from the dining room, restaurant and function room, attending to guests and preparing for the ball.

Chandeliers glistened overhead and created an atmosphere of elegant splendour. The reception was filled with chatter and energy. Gaven sensed that this Hogmanay was going to be a special one. Every year made its own mark in the castle's long history, but he felt that the air was charged with excitement.

146

The aroma of the food being cooked and served reminded Gaven that he'd been so busy he hadn't eaten a proper meal since breakfast, but that would be rectified at the lavish buffet.

Gaven went into his office behind reception and stored the bagpipes out of view, ready to be picked up at a moment's notice to play later.

Laurie wore a kilt in shades of deep blue tartan, a white shirt and tie, and a midnight blue kilt jacket with a waistcoat. He secured the silver chain on his sporran, and took a deep breath. Ready to go.

Stepping out of his cabin in his ghillie brogues, that were worn with thick woollen knee–length socks, he walked across the snow to the castle. The air was rich with the scent of the forest greenery and a snowy night.

The vast dark sky was scattered with thousands of stars and added to the grandeur of the castle.

Cars were arriving, their headlights casting dazzling beams across the castle's snow–covered gardens as a stream of cars headed to the ball.

Laurie hurried on, hoping that one of those cars belonged to Sean and that he'd be there on time to meet Sylvia when she arrived.

He stood at the side of the entrance as guests went in, smiling and chattering, dressed in their finery. And there she was, stepping out of Sean's car in a beautiful yellow evening dress that sparkled here and there with gold sequins. Sylvia's blonde hair hung softly around her shoulders, and she clasped a glittering evening bag and her sheet music.

Laurie ran out to greet her, wrapping his arm around her shoulders for warmth as she hadn't worn a coat.

Sean accompanied Muira. He wore a traditional kilt, jacket and accessories. Muira's lilac satin evening dress had a tartan sash and she'd draped a knitted lace shawl around her shoulders.

Laurie led Sylvia into the warmth of the reception.

'You look gorgeous,' Laurie said to her.

'And you look handsome in your kilt,' Sylvia told him.

Sylvia's eyes were bright with excitement as she gazed around. 'The castle's even busier than at Christmas!'

Several others arrived at the same time, including Campbell and Bee, Fyn with Aileen and Etta, Penny and Neil, and Robin and Oliver. Bradoch was there on his own, but smiling in anticipation of enjoying the evening ahead. All the men were kilted, and the ladies wore full–length evening dresses and shoes suitable for the dancing.

As they chatted, Gaven came out of his office to greet them while even more people hurried in, and the castle's guests ventured through to the function room. Everyone was offered a welcoming glass of champagne, ginger wine or a dram of whisky.

'I'll be making an announcement in the function room soon to start the ball,' Gaven told them. 'Then we'll kick the evening off with ceilidh dancing, so if you'd like to make your way through...' Gaven gestured to them.

They started to walk through, but then a voice sounded behind Etta.

'There you are!' Mullcairn said, beaming at her.

Etta looked round and smiled when she saw him.

Mullcairn gave her a huge hug and then linked her arm through his and escorted her into the function room.

'You're looking lovely, Etta.' She wore a purple satin evening dress and a tartan sash.

'And you wear your kilt well.'

'Are we going to be one of the first couples on the dance floor for the opening ceilidh dance?' Mullcairn said to her.

Etta gave his arm a squeeze. 'Oh, yes.'

'I'm booked into one of the rooms overnight,' Mullcairn said as they entered the function room. 'I'll have to drive back to Edinburgh in the morning as I've my radio show in the evening. But would you like to come up to the castle in the morning and have breakfast with me?'

Etta hesitated. 'I know that I can't compete with chef's breakfasts, but I wondered if you'd like to come to my cottage for breakfast. I need a tall, handsome dark–haired man to be my first foot on New Year's morning.'

Mullcairn's face lit up. 'I'm you're man, Etta. Though I've a few silver strands nowadays in my dark hair.'

'You're so tall, I never noticed,' Etta said playfully.

'A home–cooked breakfast at your cottage it is,' Mullcairn confirmed. 'What time should I swing by?'

'Eight?'

'I'll be there, Etta.'

Gaven saw Ian and Rose arrive and waylaid them.

'Ian, can I have a word?' Gaven began.

Thinking it was something private, Rose went over to chat to Jessy.

Ian frowned at Gaven. 'Is something wrong?'

'No, no, nothing like that. I wanted to invite you to be the castle's first footer this year.' Gaven explained what he had in mind.

Ian beamed. 'Yes, I'd be honoured to do it.'

'Grab a wee piece of coal from the scuttle beside the fire in the function room,' Gaven suggested. The first footer always arrived with something to bring good luck, warmth, a prosperous New Year. A piece of coal, shortbread or whisky were popular choices. 'Tuck the coal in your sporran and bring it in as your first foot gift.'

Ian kept smiling. 'I will, and thanks for the honour.'

'You've done so much to help with the dance lessons at the castle, encouraging ballroom dancing, hiring ballgowns for the crafting bee ladies for Christmas. I can't think of a better man as our first footer this year than yourself, Ian.'

'I've never been anyone's first footer before,' Ian revealed.

'I need you to be outside the castle on the rundown to midnight, so that you'll be the first to step inside after the bells,' Gaven told him.

Ian nodded. 'I'll stand outside for a few minutes before the old year comes to a close.'

'Walter, Jessy and I will keep you right,' said Gaven. 'I'll play the bagpipes to ring in the New Year, and fireworks will be set off. At this point, the castle's front door will be open, as will the patio doors and a few windows. It's a tradition for the air to blow through to cast the old year out and the fresh one in. After all of this, the front door will be closed in readiness for you knocking on it as our first footer.'

Ian understood and was eager to participate. It added something even more memorable to the whole event for him. His first New Year ball at the castle, a new life in the village, and a new romance with Rose.

'Gare will be there to film you chapping on the castle door,' said Gaven. 'As I'll be outside this year playing the bagpipes, and Walter is setting off the fireworks, I've chosen chef to officially greet you when you step into reception and accept the wee bit of coal. We'll put the event up later on our website.'

'Wonderful,' said Ian.

'And you're welcome to invite Rose to stand in reception so that she's included in the video,' Gaven added.

'I'll do that,' Ian said eagerly.

Walter waved over to Gaven, an indication that it was time to start the ball.

Ian clasped Rose's hand and told her the news as they all hurried through to the function room.

The buffet tables stretched along one side of the room, laden with a delicious selection of food. The Christmas tree was lit and the fire provided plenty of warmth. People were milling around and Gaven made his way through them to give his announcement.

'Welcome to our New Year ball,' Gaven began. 'I hope you enjoy the ceilidh and ballroom dancing. And the buffet. The dancing will continue until almost midnight when we'll wave farewell to the old year and welcome in the New Year with celebratory fireworks and traditional bagpipe playing.'

'We hear you're ringing in the New Year playing the bagpipes yourself, Gaven,' one of the guests called out, causing others to chatter excitedly about the laird performing.

'I am,' Gaven confirmed. 'We have lots of fun and entertainment for you. So I'd like to invite you to take to the floor for the opening ceilidh dance — a lively reel. Happy Hogmanay everyone!'

The applause and cheers were soon drowned out by the sound of the traditional music as the dancing began.

Gaven was at the heart of it, dancing with the castle's guests and those from the local village.

Etta and Mullcairn were one of the first couples to join in the reel, and Walter had pulled Jessy into the throng.

Ian spun Rose around the lively reel and linked arms and hands with others including Penny and Neil and Aileen and Fyn.

Everyone danced with everyone else and as the first tune ended, the next one began seamlessly, causing the reel to continue.

Sylvia held on to Laurie's hand tight as they twirled around, then clasped hands with Gaven, then Oliver and Bradoch.

Gare stood beside the Christmas tree filming the fun, but was then pulled into the dancing by Jessy.

'Put your camera down for a few minutes, Gare,' Jessy called to him. 'Come and dance.'

Gare tucked his camera under the Christmas tree and then whirled around the dance floor with the others.

After four reels and two jigs, some of the revellers took a breather and tucked into the lavish delights of the buffet.

'I'll be back in a minute,' Ian said to Rose. 'Save me a slice of chef's savoury pie with puff pastry.'

Ian ran off, winding through the busy dance floor, but got caught up in a jig, pulled in by Muira and Bee, then he skip–stepped away tactfully over to the fire.

Beside the log fire burning in the large hearth was an old–fashioned bronze coat scuttle. Ian lifted a piece of coal from the scuttle and tucked it into his sporran.

Dashing back over to the buffet, Ian added a spoonful of mashed potatoes and turnip to go with his pie.

Rose had a slice of the pie too with roast potatoes.

Sean playfully nudged Ian aside. 'Leave a slice for Muira and me, Ian.'

'And us!' Sylvia cut–in, sidling up with Laurie.

Etta and Mullcairn joined them.

'I've a liking for clootie dumpling,' Mullcairn revealed. 'Do we have to eat the buffet in the right order? Savouries first and then puddings.'

'No rules tonight, Mullcairn,' Etta announced and dished up a portion of clootie dumpling for him. 'Custard or cream with it?'

'A wee slather of both,' said Mullcairn, lifting a spoon to tuck in.

Etta put a haggis vol–au–vent on her plate and side scoops of neeps and tatties.

Laughing, they all enjoyed the buffet, the company and the dancing.

Gare went by filming the fun while eating a haggis sausage roll.

Seeing his brother eating it, Fyn wanted one, and Walter had to point them out to him amid the wide selection of items available on the buffet tables.

'I love these,' Fyn mumbled through a mouthful of flaky pastry.

Aileen shook her head at him and smiled while helping herself to a slice of chef's quiche topped with cherry tomatoes, peppers and greentails.

By now, Mullcairn had worked his way backwards to one of the salmon dishes.

Etta had moved on to a slice of rich fruitcake.

'You'd better grab something to eat,' Walter said to Gaven. 'Chef will top up the buffet, but you'd better get in there.'

Gaven laughed, and lifted a portion of the savoury pie with roast potatoes.

He'd barely had a chance to finish it when the first song began for the ballroom dances.

Putting their plates down, Gaven and the others stepped on to the dance floor for the first waltz.

Sylvia whispered to Laurie. 'That's my cue to go through to the piano bar. I'm playing the next few songs for the ballroom dancing.'

'I'll come through to the piano bar with you,' said Laurie.

'Are you sure? I'm happy for you to stay here and enjoy the dancing.'

Laurie smiled at her. 'I'd rather be with you while you're playing the piano, unless I'll put you off.'

'No, you won't,' Sylvia said cheerily. 'Come on, I've got my sheet music stored in the piano stool.'

Sylvia and Laurie hurried away together leaving everyone waltzing around.

The piano bar was fairly quiet as people were through in the function room dancing. Sylvia sat down and set up her sheet music ready to play a beautifully romantic song, a popular piece from yesteryear.

As before, Walter had set up the sound system to pipe the piano music through to the function room.

Sylvia could hear the current song finishing, and waited for Gaven to announce her performance.

'And now, we have a live performance of music from Sylvia in the piano bar,' Gaven announced. 'Sylvia is playing a wonderful selection of songs for us this evening. Thank you, Sylvia!'

Hearing her cue, as she'd agreed with Gaven, Sylvia began playing.

Even though Laurie had heard her perform before and knew what a wonderful classically trained pianist she was, his heart soared watching her fingers glide across the keys of the baby grand piano.

Go, Sylvia! Laurie thought to himself.

Her sheet music was propped up in front of her, but she glanced over at Laurie sitting nearby and smiled at him while continuing to play with skill and heart. The sequins in her dress sparkled under the light of the chandelier.

Couples waltzed around the dance floor, hearing the melodic music playing over the sound system, and a few people, including Muira and Sean, popped through for a moment to watch Sylvia play the piano.

'She's a magnificent pianist,' Sean whispered to Muira.

'Sylvia always had talent,' Muira whispered back.

Sean kept his voice down. 'Look at the way Laurie's gazing at her. He's well smitten.'

Muira nodded and smiled, and then they headed back through to the function room to waltz to the beautiful music.

CHAPTER TWELVE

'Wearing a kilt for the foxtrot adds swing to my sway, don't you think?' Ian said as he danced with Rose.

'I think you've got plenty of sway in your foxtrot with or without your kilt,' Rose told him, smiling.

Ian pretended to be shocked. 'Dancing without my kilt? That's a step too far,' he teased her.

Even though she knew he was winding her up, she felt a blush across her cheeks. 'You're a rascal.'

Ian held her close and then dipped her as he replied. 'But I'm your rascal.'

Rose laughed, and then he righted her and they continued to foxtrot around the dance floor.

Sylvia was still playing in the piano bar, but her performance was drawing to a close.

Walter hurried through from the function room and peered in at her.

'*This is the last song*,' Sylvia mouthed to Walter as she continued to play a traditional number that was a popular choice for a romantic waltz or slow foxtrot.

Walter gave Sylvia the thumbs up and ran back through to the function room in readiness to start playing music from his list. An upbeat song was next, and the plan was that guests would now begin samba dancing.

Ian had a basic idea of the playlist order, but he could change from a waltz to a samba with ease, so as Sylvia's song finished on a lingering note, and the upbeat number began, he hit the samba rhythm without skipping a beat.

A few couples followed Ian's lead as he danced with Rose, including Sean and Muira, Campbell and Bee, and Etta and Mullcairn.

'I don't know what I'm dancing,' Mullcairn said to Etta as he threw himself into the swing of it. 'But my hips haven't moved like this in a long time.'

'About time they did then,' Etta told him, showing him the moves she'd learned from Ian. 'This is the samba.'

'Okay,' said Mullcairn, following Etta's lead when she showed him her voltas. 'They've got plenty of bounce in them,' Etta told him.

'Gaun yersel, Etta,' Mullcairn cheered.

'You'll need to teach us the rumba and the salsa,' Jessy called over to Ian.

'Pencil those lessons in for the spring,' Ian replied, expecting to be taken up on his offer.

Sylvia folded her sheet music and put it away for safe keeping in the piano stool intending to take it home with her later.

'You played wonderfully,' Laurie told her, coming over to escort her through to the function room to join the others.

Sylvia ran her fingers along the top of the piano lid as she closed it to protect the keys. 'One day, I've promised myself that I'll have a piano like this, and a house with room to play it in.'

Laurie felt the urge to tell her that this promise was due to be fulfilled, but bit back his comments. The timing wasn't right. Again, time was against him. But he hoped to sort this out soon.

'It sounds like the dancing has notched up a few gears. Do you want to go through and join in?' Laurie held his hand out to Sylvia.

Smiling, she clasped his hand. 'Yes, I can relax now that I've played without messing up the songs.'

'I don't think that relaxing is on tonight's schedule,' Laurie said as they walked in to find the dance floor jumping with people doing the samba or variations of that theme.

Sylvia laughed, and they joined in with the fun of the dancing.

'When do you perform?' Sylvia said to Laurie as he danced close to her for the samba rolls.

'After the samba and another three rounds of ceilidh dancing.'

Sylvia smiled. She was eager to hear Laurie perform.

'But we'll grab another bite to eat at the buffet soon,' said Laurie. Apart from singing and playing guitar, he was fuelling up in readiness for playing the bagpipes outside in the snowy night. Glancing out the patio doors, it looked like a winter wonderland.

Dancing the samba, Laurie and Sylvia then joined in the first ceilidh reel before heading over to the buffet.

Having something to eat, they chatted about the songs Laurie was about to perform.

'They're a selection from my past two albums,' Laurie told her.

'Are you playing your acoustic or electric guitar?' said Sylvia.

159

'Both. Mainly electric. The red one. I played it on one of my last tours and these are the songs I performed, so I thought it would be appropriate.'

Sylvia agreed. 'I love that you keep some of the guitars from your past tours.'

'They show that they've been played from the scuffs and scratches, but they still sound great and I feel comfortable playing them.' Laurie checked the time. 'I'd better get ready.'

'I'll be cheering you on.' Sylvia kissed him and smiled.

Laurie headed through to collect his guitars from the small storeroom.

Leaving the bagpipes where they were, he carried the two guitars, one electric, one acoustic, through to the back of the function room and started to set up to perform.

Walter looked over at him, ready to fade the dance music as the third reel finished.

Gaven stepped forward. 'Now we have a special performance from Laurie. He's going to sing a few songs from his last two albums.' Gaven then started the applause.

People stopped dancing to watch Laurie.

He slung the strap of his electric guitar around his neck and started to play the opening riff of the first song. One of his top–selling numbers, guests recognised what he was about to play and started clapping, eager to hear him sing live.

'Remember to enjoy your dancing,' Laurie announced, encouraging them to dance while he performed.

Ian was the first to get the dancing going again, taking Rose in hold and doing a lively variation of a waltz, moving in time to the upbeat song.

Taking Ian's lead, couples quickly joined in, and soon the dance floor was filled with people dancing while Laurie sang and played his guitar.

Sylvia danced with Bradoch, and then she danced with Sean and Gaven, while enjoying Laurie's performance.

The sound of his electric guitar notched up the party dancing, and when he finished the songs as scheduled, guests wanted him to play some more, so he obliged, changing guitars a couple of times to suit the songs.

Finally, Sylvia took a few moments on her own, standing beside the Christmas tree, to watch Laurie. She loved to hear him sing. And she loved him dearly.

Laurie kept the songs upbeat until the last one. He smiled over at her standing at the Christmas tree and his deep voice resonated across to her. 'This song is for Sylvia.'

Everyone looked over at her, and she found herself blushing.

'It's a new song for the album I'm working on,' said Laurie. 'Here's to a happy new year and new love and romance.'

The guests applauded, and Gaven nodded over to Laurie, encouraging him to do this, and then there was silence as he started to play...

The opening riff played on the electric guitar had a soulful quality that hit all the right notes to create a feeling of longing. The atmosphere in the function room was electric, matching the rich tones of Laurie's song.

From the opening riff, the song broke into a memorable first verse, and Laurie could tell from the atmosphere that he was right. This song was special. He'd sensed it the moment he'd played it in his cabin. A standout number for the album, and one that he'd play for many years to come.

But there was nothing like playing a song for the first time after creating it. Hearing it for himself was fine, but seeing the faces of the people listening, their reaction, was touching. The song itself was a moving melody, but then built to a hopeful ending, like a new beginning by the final verse. Heads started to nod as he repeated the chorus. The song resonated fast with the audience of friends and familiar strangers alike.

Sylvia stood there listening, feeling quite emotional, hearing the words on a personal note, as if Laurie was telling their story. A story that others would share when it was released on the next album.

Laurie had done it again, Sylvia thought to herself. He'd created another hit on his already wonderful album of new songs. And she felt part of it.

Couples slow danced to the song, and Laurie saw many of them gazing lovingly at each other as they waltzed close. Long–time loves and recent romantics danced as if the song was part of their story together too.

I love you from the lilac dawnlight
Until the sky's a midnight blue
A thousand silver stars above
My heart belongs to you

My sweetest love...

As the final notes from the guitar resonated and Laurie stopped playing, everyone lingered in the romance of the moment, and then applauded and cheered.

Picking up his guitars, Laurie wound his way through the guests, many of them smiling, commenting on how much they enjoyed his performance, and made his way out of the function room and through to store his guitars again.

In the privacy of the storeroom he took a few moments to settle himself, to think through his forthcoming performance on the bagpipes. He took them out of the bag and sat them on the table ready to be picked up soon. Then he turned the light off and went back through to join Sylvia and the others.

Everyone continued to dance, and there was a sense of excitement during the last hour of the year.

'My heart feels so excited,' Sylvia confided to Laurie as they sipped glasses of ginger wine, taking a moment to stand by the patio doors and gaze out at the snow glistening in the light–glow from the castle. 'I love Hogmanay, but there's something special that I sense this year.' She smiled and shrugged. 'It's probably all the excitement recently leading up to this evening. And your wonderful songs, particularly the last one. No one has ever dedicated a song to me before, so that's like a fairytale come true.' She could hear herself babbling, but Laurie made no move to interrupt her, so she continued. 'But there's something special in the air tonight...' She shrugged again and sipped her ginger wine.

Laurie agreed with her, but he couldn't tell her, not yet...

'I'm away to sort out the fireworks,' Walter said to Gaven. A couple of the staff were on hand to help him, but he mainly lit the fireworks himself.

Gaven nodded firmly and checked the time. 'Not long now until the bells. I'll be out soon.'

Walter hurried away. Jessy noticed, taking that as her cue to help with the preparations, but everyone was so busy enjoying themselves that they continued to dance and have something to eat and drink at the buffet. Chef and his staff had kept the buffet topped up, but soon the kitchen would be sizzling as the New Year breakfast was prepared.

It was a tradition at the castle that after the bells at midnight, the ball continued well into the early hours of the morning. A tasty breakfast was served before the dawn, often around two in the morning, and comprised of sausages, Lorne square sausage, eggs cooked several ways, tattie scones galore and other items to fill the guests' plates, along with loads of tea. Coffee, hot chocolate and other drinks were available and a glass of whisky for those still indulging.

Gaven had organised a mini bus to take guests home to the village later on, and they were welcome to leave their cars parked at the castle. Often, those from the village organised their own transport.

The task of announcing the rundown to midnight fell to Jessy this year as Gaven would be outside to play the bagpipes.

Jessy stood beside the Christmas tree in readiness. She'd seen the laird announce this for many years, and was happy to do the honours this time.

Ian checked the time and glanced at Rose. 'I need to head outside now.'

Rose intended staying in the function room with Etta, Muira and others for the announcement, and go out to see the fireworks, and then be in the reception for Ian's first footer arrival.

Sean noticed a few key people making their moves and whispered to Muira. 'I notice that Walter, Gaven and others have disappeared. They must be getting ready for the chimes.'

Muira stood close to Sean. 'I'm so glad you joined in this year.'

Sean put his arm around her shoulders. 'So am I, Muira.'

Campbell and Bee came over to join them, as did Etta, Mullcairn and Rose.

'I'm away outside now,' Gare said to Fyn and Aileen. 'I need to be set up to film the bagpipes being played, and the fireworks.'

'We'll be out soon to see the display,' Fyn told Gare.

Neil, Penny, Robin and Oliver walked over to join Fyn and Aileen, chatting about the forthcoming performance on the bagpipes from Gaven.

Laurie pulled Sylvia close. 'I'm backing Gaven on the bagpipes,' he confided.

Sylvia looked surprised and delighted.

'I didn't say because I want Gaven to get the credit for stepping up and doing this,' Laurie explained.

Sylvia understood, but she was pleased that Laurie was playing too. 'I'll be outside watching you play.'

Laurie leaned down and kissed her. 'See you in the New Year.' And then he ran off to pick up the bagpipes and head outside.

Sylvia went over to Jessy. 'I didn't bring a coat with me. I should've, but I got in such a tizzy getting ready for the ball—'

'There are spare coats and shawls for guests to use in the cloakroom.' Jessy led her through to pick one before it was time for the announcement.

On a separate rail in the cloakroom there was a selection of coats, jackets, shawls and other warm accessories that were available for guests to help themselves.

Jessy quickly helped Sylvia find something suitable.

'Here's a lovely warm shawl, but it's an evening shawl with a bit of glitter yarn in the knitted weave.' Jessy held it up.

Sylvia clasped it instantly. 'This is ideal. Thanks, Jessy.'

'Now, hurry up, it's nearly time for the rundown.' Jessy urged Sylvia to scamper back through to the function room.

Sylvia joined Muira, Sean and the others while Jessy went over to the Christmas tree to make the announcement. They had an old–fashioned clock set up that ticked the seconds away to the midnight hour.

Other members of staff had opened the patio doors and other doors and windows to let the cold air blow through, pushing out the old year and refreshing it with the new one.

'It's time now to say goodbye to the old year,' Jessy announced, as Gaven always phrased it. 'So can I invite you to join in with me as we count down the seconds...'

The guests' voices sounded in unison, filling the room with a hearty tone.

'Ten, nine, eight, seven...' the voices roared.

Sylvia's heart beat with excitement for this, and for Laurie.

'Three, two...one!' The voices shouted the final three seconds and then there were cheers galore, hugs, kisses, everyone wishing everyone else a Happy New Year.

Sylvia kissed and hugged Muira, Sean and a couple of others and then hurried away, throwing the shawl around her shoulders as she ran through reception and out into the snowy night.

Walter's fireworks had just started soaring into the sky, illuminating it in vibrant colours of sparkling light that for once outshone the stars.

And there was Gaven, standing in the snow a few feet away from the front entrance of the castle, playing the bagpipes. The first traditional song rang clear in the crisp, cold air.

Gaven was determined to play well, and against expectations, his fingers didn't feel the cold, and his rendition sounded excellent.

Glancing round, he saw Laurie standing further away in the snow, pleased that his back–up was there as promised.

167

Laurie didn't play a note while Gare recorded the laird playing the bagpipes to give a traditional welcome to the New Year.

As Gaven finished the first song, and began to play the second one they'd rehearsed, Laurie started to play in the near distance.

Together, their playing had a wonderful quality that stirred the onlookers. The majority of the guests had gathered at the front entrance, standing outside to enjoy the performance of Gaven and Laurie.

Walter's firework display provided a magnificent backdrop to their playing, and every moment was captured on video by Gare.

Ian had his arm around Rose, and even though she wore a warm coat, she snuggled into him, loving every second of this special time.

Glancing around, she saw that other couples were standing close together, including Penny and Neil, Robin and Oliver and Fyn and Aileen.

Mullcairn had Etta in a warm hug as she stood beside him, watching the display of fireworks and music.

Bradoch stood in the midst of his friends and the guests, thoroughly enjoying the evening.

Muira and Sean were beside Sylvia, and they all exchanged smiles while listening to the bagpipe music.

On the third song, Laurie played a descant to Gaven's main tune, creating a memorable and melodic sound that impressed and delighted the guests.

Sparkles of gold, vibrant pink, lilac, silver and turquoise from the fireworks rained down in the dark sky, disappearing into the air, arousing cheers from the onlookers.

'What a display from Walter,' Campbell said to Sean.

'Aye.' Sean nodded. 'And what wonderful bagpipe playing.'

Others nearby agreed.

Gaven had been right. It was going to be a Hogmanay to remember.

Sylvia was right too. There was a feeling of something special in the cold night air. A shiver of anticipation ran through her, and she pulled the glittering shawl closer around her shoulders. But it wasn't the snowy air that had made her shiver. It was a feeling that something special was about to happen soon.

CHAPTER THIRTEEN

Fireworks soared into the night sky as Gaven played another song on the bagpipes. The traditional song was one he'd played for years in the past, and he'd rehearsed it at the music studio, keeping it as back–up if he needed other songs to perform. He saw the smiling faces of those standing in the snow outside the front entrance of the castle, and this gave him the confidence to continue playing for them while they celebrated the New Year.

Gare stood outside the castle filming everything from the performance to the fireworks display.

Laurie stopped playing and put his bagpipes away in the case he'd brought with him. He sat it down on the snow out of the way. Standing on his own, away from where Gaven was continuing to play, the snow–covered trees at the edge of the estate shielded him from the bitter cold.

While everyone watched the fireworks display, Laurie took the ring box out of his sporran. His heart thundered with excitement and anticipation for what he was about to do.

Laurie waved across to where Sylvia was standing at the front of the castle and beckoned her to come and join him.

Seeing that Laurie had stopped playing the bagpipes, Sylvia smiled and hurried over, wanting to be the first one to wish him a Happy New Year. Her flat pumps pressed into the soft snow, but it wasn't too deep so she felt fine as she walked over to him. She pulled the shawl around her shoulders for warmth. The glitter in the knit caught the light, as did the sequins on her dress.

Laurie smiled to himself, watching the sparkling figure hurrying across the snow towards him. Do this right, he thought. Make it special.

As she got closer, Laurie knelt down on one knee in the snow and held the ring box in his hand.

Sylvia jolted, realising what was about to happen, clearly taken aback.

She walked towards him as he smiled up at her.

The air was filled with the scent of a snowy night, the fireworks and the greenery from the surrounding forest.

'Sylvia, I love you,' Laurie began. He opened the velvet box to reveal the dazzling diamond ring.

She gasped, seeing the three diamonds sparkle in the white gold band.

Her heart thundered in anticipation of his proposal.

'Will you marry me, Sylvia?' Laurie's deep voice resonated in the cold night air.

'Yes, I will,' she said, her voice unsteady with joyous emotion. 'I love you, Laurie.'

He gently placed the ring on her finger, and then stood up.

Sylvia blinked, seeing the ring sparkle in the nightglow. 'It's a beautiful ring. I love it.'

Laurie pulled her close, wrapping her in his loving embrace. 'And I love you.' He kissed her, long and lingering, with romance and all the love in his heart.

Then he held her close as they stood watching the fireworks illuminate the sky.

'Happy New Year,' he said.

Sylvia smiled at him. 'Happy New Year, Laurie.'

He kissed her again.

Wrapping her in his arms, they watched the last of the fireworks soar across the night sky, raining sparkles of gold, blue, silver and pink down on the snowscape.

Everyone was now getting ready for Ian's first footing. Staff ensured that guests standing outside the castle stayed there while the front door was closed.

Ian then took the piece of coal from his sporran, walked up to the castle's door and knocked on it.

Chef opened the door and welcomed Ian into the reception.

Ian presented the coal to chef and then they shook hands and wished each other a Happy New Year.

Gare filmed this from outside the front door.

The ceremony complete, guests were then able to enter the castle.

Rose walked in after Gare and she was included in the video of Ian shaking hands with other guests and staff. Ian then clasped hands with Rose to ensure she was part of the event.

Gaven strode in carrying the bagpipes and was cheered and applauded. He put the bagpipes in his office and then urged everyone to go back through to the function room to continue the dancing and help themselves to a celebratory drink from the buffet.

Laurie and Sylvia were the last couple to walk into the function room. They went over to Muira and Sean.

Sylvia held up her hand to show them the ring.

Muira squealed with delight. 'I'm so happy for the two of you.'

'Congratulations to you,' Sean told them.

There were hugs and kisses all round, and within a few minutes the word had circulated that Laurie had proposed to Sylvia.

Several of their friends hurried over to congratulate them. Glasses of champagne were raised in a toast to Laurie and Sylvia, and lots of pictures were taken of the happy couple.

A few of the crafting bee ladies tried on Sylvia's ring and made a wish.

Then Laurie took Sylvia on to the dance floor and they joined in a lively reel.

Amid the excitement, Gare stood beside the Christmas tree, reviewing his video. He was pleased to see that he'd filmed what he needed, especially Gaven and Laurie playing the bagpipes, and the fireworks display. And then he saw something special. He'd inadvertently captured Laurie proposing to Sylvia. While the fireworks soared overhead, and Gaven played the bagpipes, there in the background was the proposal.

Gare looked over to the dance floor, searching for Laurie and Sylvia. He waved to them.

They stopped dancing and wound their way across to the Gare.

'I was filming the fireworks,' Gare began. 'But I've captured the two of you in the background. If you want, I'll give you a copy. And I'll keep it private if you don't want others to see.'

'I'd love a copy,' said Sylvia. 'And I'm happy for others to see it.'

Laurie agreed. 'This is great. Thanks, Gare.'

Delighted that they could share the proposal, Laurie and Sylvia went back to join in the dancing.

Ian whirled Rose around, and then she danced with Gaven. Campbell danced with Muira while Sean partnered with Bee. There were cheers as everyone enjoyed the fast–moving reel.

Taking a break from the lively reels, Laurie and Sylvia went over to the buffet to indulge in another glass of champagne, and were joined by Mullcairn and Etta.

'Congratulations to the two of you,' Mullcairn began. 'Are you keeping your engagement private? Or could I mention it on my radio show tomorrow night? I'm going to be telling listeners about celebrating Hogmanay at the castle, and Gaven playing the bagpipes. It would be wonderful to reveal the news about you and Sylvia.'

'You're welcome to tell your listeners,' said Laurie. 'We're not keeping our engagement a secret.'

Mullcairn smiled. 'Great. It'll be an exciting piece of news. Make sure you listen in.'

'We will,' Sylvia assured Mullcairn.

Etta admired the diamond ring. 'It's gorgeous.'

'I keep looking at it,' Sylvia said, giggling. 'I didn't expect this.'

'I'd been planning to propose at Christmas,' Laurie revealed. 'But the house and studio weren't finished, so I had to change my plans.'

'New Year is perfect,' Sylvia told Laurie.

'Did you get down on one knee?' Mullcairn said to Laurie. 'Any details I can share with my listeners?'

'I did,' Laurie confirmed. 'Outside in the snow while Gaven was playing another song on the bagpipes and the fireworks display was still going on.'

'Gare has the proposal on video,' Sylvia said to Mullcairn and Etta. 'He's going to give us a copy.'

Mullcairn looked around. 'Where is Gare? I'd like a wee peek at the proposal so I can explain the details on the show.'

'Gare's standing near the Christmas tree,' said Laurie, peering over at him.

While Etta made a wish on Sylvia's engagement ring, Laurie and Mullcairn went to talk to Gare and have a look at the video.

'I'll be able to describe the scene outside the castle in the snow,' Mullcairn said, taking in the details. 'People love your music, Laurie, and they'll be keen to hear all about your engagement to Sylvia.'

Laurie and Sylvia, and Mullcairn and Etta then joined in the dancing.

A mix of ceilidh reels and jigs, foxtrot, samba and waltzing continued well into the night as everyone enjoyed the New Year ball.

The music finally changed to a slower pace and couples began to waltz around the dance floor.

The romantic waltz was the perfect dance for the newly engaged couple, and Sylvia smiled up at Laurie as he held her close. He leaned down and kissed her, and then they continued to slow dance to the romantic music.

Chef and his staff cleared away part of the buffet and started to replace it with the breakfast food.

The aroma of hot buttered toast alerted guests that breakfast was now being served, tempting them to help themselves to the Lorne sausage, haggis, tattie scones, grilled tomatoes, slices of Scottish fruit pudding, fresh baked soda scones, Scottish morning rolls, slices of plain loaf, eggs scrambled or fried, baked beans, cheddar and other savoury delights.

Sylvia picked up a slice of hot buttered toast and chatted to Muira, still excited about being engaged. The buffet was abuzz with chatter as everyone selected what they wanted.

Gaven put a slice of Lorne sausage on a buttered roll.

Seeing the laird's choice, Laurie joined him.

'I think I'll have one of those,' said Laurie. 'It looks tasty.' He added tomato sauce to his.

Gaven drank a mouthful of tea. 'I'm fuelling up for swimming in the loch.'

By now, Sean, Campbell and Ian had gathered round to grab a roll with the square sliced sausage.

Laurie frowned. 'Swimming? Tonight?'

Gaven shook his head. 'No, in the morning.' He checked the time. 'Though technically it is morning, but not until mid–morning, around eleven is when I always go for a swim on the first day of the year. Anyone can join me if they want.'

'I always go,' Walter chimed–in.

'Isn't it freezing?' said Ian.

'Oh, yes,' Gaven said, making it sound icy cold. He bit into his roll and sausage.

'I'll join in,' Bee piped–up, causing Campbell to jolt.

Bee was a seasoned swimmer. Her slight figure belied the powerful swimmer she was. Raised in the north of Scotland, the Shetlands and the Orkney islands, swimming in the wild sea in all weathers was something she'd always loved.

Campbell spoke up. 'I'll go. I love swimming. It'll be a great way to celebrate the forthcoming year.'

'Count me in,' Sean added, and glanced at Muira.

'I'm working in the sweet shop,' said Muira, smiling that she had a valid excuse.

'So am I,' Sylvia added.

'Okay, I'll go,' Ian said decisively. He looked at Rose.

'I'll wave to you from the edge of the loch,' Rose said with a smile.

'I've joined in before, so I'll do it again,' said Fyn. 'My shop is never busy on New Year's morning.'

'I'll be busy starting my January sale tomorrow in the quilt shop,' said Aileen.

Bradoch looked like he would've joined in. 'Folk expect my bakery to be open all morning. But I'll take part in the sledging at night whenever that happens.'

'Soon,' said Walter. 'What about you, Jessy? Going in for a paddle this year?'

'Maybe,' said Jessy, undecided. 'But someone has to tend to the castle.'

'Jump in the car with Walter and me,' Gaven encouraged her. 'The staff can handle things for a wee while. We won't be gone that long.'

'Okay, I'll do it,' said Jessy. 'But just a paddle at the edge.'

Sylvia glanced out the patio windows. 'It's snowing!'

'The loch will be extra cold,' said Laurie. And then decided to join in.

'I like a wee swim in the loch,' said Gaven. 'I've done this for years.'

They continued to enjoy the breakfast buffet, and Gaven mingled with the guests, and organised the final few dances to round off the ball.

Walter set up the music as Gaven made the closing announcement.

'I hope you all enjoyed our New Year ball,' Gaven began. 'We're concluding the evening with a few popular dances, including a romantic waltz. And congratulations to Laurie and Sylvia on their engagement.'

A cheer went up, and as the music began, the dance floor started to fill up.

The lights were dimmed to create a romantic atmosphere, with mainly the twinkle lights on the Christmas tree and the chandeliers illuminating the room.

'Shall we?' Ian said to Rose, holding his hand out to her.

Rose began to slow foxtrot with Ian to the music.

Laurie swept Sylvia on to the dance floor and they waltzed under the sparkling chandeliers.

Sylvia was due to head back to the sweet shop. Sean had kept to soft drinks so that he could drive Muira and Sylvia home.

'I know you're working in the morning at the shop,' Laurie said as they danced. 'But I want to invite you to see the house and the studio soon.'

'I'd like that,' she said.

Holding her close, they continued to waltz around until the final slow dance, finishing in a loving embrace.

People began to filter out of the function room, guests heading to their rooms, and others organising lifts from their friends back down to the village, or taking the mini bus available.

The front entrance to the castle was alive with activity, lights and chatter as everyone poured out into the night.

It was snowing, and as the flakes fluttered down around them, Laurie kissed Sylvia goodnight. She had the shawl wrapped around her shoulders, but he didn't want her to stand for long in the freezing cold, even though he wished they could extend the evening.

'Can I have the ring box?' she said. 'I'd like to keep it for storing my ring.'

Laurie gave her the little velvet box, and she clasped it and smiled at him.

'I'll call you tomorrow,' he promised.

'Enjoy your swim in the loch.'

'I'm not sure what I've let myself in for.'

They kissed goodnight, and then she hurried over to Sean's car and got in the back seat.

Waving to Laurie, they drove off.

Laurie stood there for a moment, smiling to himself, feeling hopeful, and then he went into the castle to pick up his instruments.

Gaven was in reception bidding guests goodnight, and Laurie slipped by unnoticed into the storeroom, collected the guitars and the bagpipes, then headed back out.

Walter came hurrying after him. 'Laurie!'

He turned around.

'We're having a sledging evening tomorrow night,' Walter told him. 'I've just spoken to Gaven, and we'll have it around seven. I hope you'll join in.'

'Yes, I'd love to,' Laurie confirmed.

'We'll have an afternoon event soon and another evening of sledging,' Walter added, and then waved and hurried back into reception.

Laurie walked through the snow carrying the instruments, keen to enjoy the sledging, but feeling his schedule fill up. He needed to plan when to have the special evening at his house for Sylvia.

As the snow started to fall heavier, he stepped up his pace to reach the cabin. It had been quite a night.

Unlocking the door, he stepped inside, put the instruments down, and shook the snowflakes from his kilt jacket as he took it off and hung it up.

Snow fell outside his bedroom window as he took his tie off and unbuttoned his shirt, all the while thinking about Sylvia. She'd accepted his proposal. Now he wanted to show her the house and the piano in the studio.

Climbing into bed, he didn't even want to think about how late at night it was, or that he was due to go swimming in the loch. He just wanted to lie there and relax, watch the snow and get some sleep. Another busy and exciting day was ahead.

Sylvia hung her evening dress up and got ready for bed.

Tucked under the covers, she gazed out at the snowy night.

The engagement ring sparkled on her finger in the night glow. Reaching over to her bedside table, she took it off and put it safely in the box.

Her heart fluttered every time she thought about Laurie proposing in the snow. What a night!

Snuggling down, she finally fell asleep.

CHAPTER FOURTEEN

Laurie woke up to a tranquil frosted dawn that was trying to bring light to the new morning. Barely any glow shone in the deep cobalt sky and a scattering of stars were still glittering as the night finally gave way to the first day of January.

He sat up and checked the time on his phone. A handful of hours had slipped through his slumbering fingers, but a new song jarred him awake and he got out of bed to capture it before it faded like the night was doing.

Throwing on a pair of jeans and a jumper for warmth, he used the fastest way to sharpen his creative thoughts and hurried through to the living room and then opened the cabin's door.

Breathing in the cold fresh air, he gazed over at the castle in the distance. Hardly any lights were on inside, only a couple of lanterns at the entrance, and the front door was closed against the elements. Even the lights on the Christmas tree were turned off, though the snow sparkled with enough of nature's illumination to make the castle look like it belonged in a winter fairytale.

Everything was so still that he felt inclined to stifle the sound of his breathing so as not to disturb the rare quietude. Not a branch creaking under the weight of the newly sprinkled snow, no icicles dripping their glistening drops on to the ground, not a leaf falling or a breeze wafting past anything...

Laurie breathed in deeply, starting to hear the music, the melody, clearer this time, remembering the song he'd played in his half–slumber. The notes sounded beautiful, different from the other songs he was creating for his album. And that was what he needed. Something different, but in tune with his style of music.

Leaving the cabin door ajar, he grabbed his phone from the pocket of his jeans, and began humming the tune, singing the hint of lyrics that accompanied it. It was the fastest way to capture something so elusive that it could be gone by the time he'd set up his keyboard or guitar to record himself playing.

He didn't have the whole song, just snatches, but they were the ones he needed. The opening riff, the theme of the lyrics, the beat of the first verse and the chorus. The heart of the song was all there. Something he could build on. And he would. Inspiration was what he'd wanted when he came to stay in the cabin for a creative break. And that's exactly what he had right now.

The dawn wasn't making any great impact on the darkness, and anyone that had danced the night away at the ball would surely be sound asleep. The castle always had an early start, especially when breakfasts were served from seven–thirty in the morning. But it wasn't close to that time. Not yet.

Having recorded what he needed on his phone, Laurie then went inside, set up his keyboard and guitar, and spent the next hour in the seclusion of his cabin playing and working on the new song.

Mullcairn checked out of the castle in the morning. He wore comfy casuals and a Fair Isle jumper he'd previously bought from Etta. His kilt was packed in his overnight bag.

Stepping outside, he defrosted his car, put his bag in the boot, and then drove down the forest road to Etta's cottage just before eight in the morning.

She'd told him exactly where her cottage was situated overlooking the loch.

And there it was, a traditional cottage, one of several dotted around the hillside.

He parked his car and walked across the snow—covered garden to her front door and knocked.

'It's open,' Etta called through to him from the kitchen. 'Come on in.'

Hearing her voice, Mullcairn kicked the snow from his boots and stepped inside. The delicious aroma of breakfast being cooked wafted from the kitchen along the hall.

Mullcairn followed the aroma and the sound of Etta busily preparing a tasty breakfast.

'Happy New Year, Etta!' He held up a bottle of whisky he'd bought from the castle's piano bar as his first foot gift.

Etta quickly wiped her hands and smiled at him. 'A Happy New Year to you too. Thank you for being my first foot this year.'

She accepted the gift and put the bottle of whisky on a shelf while she continued to cook the scrambled eggs, tattie scones and Lorne sausage. The bread was already buttered and plates were set on the kitchen table.

'Sit yourself down,' she said, serving up their breakfast.

Mullcairn looked around the cosy kitchen. 'This is a lovely cottage.' He liked the homely atmosphere and the view of the hillside from the kitchen window.

Etta poured their tea and sat down to join him. 'I like it. It suits me, nice and cosy and comfortable. Overlooking the loch. Two minutes walk to the main street. A view of the castle's turrets. I often have my knitting bee nights here. I'll show you the living room where I do my knitting and quilting before you go.'

'Aye, I'm interested to see where you do all your knitting.'

Mullcairn tucked into the home cooked breakfast, knowing he'd made the right choice to join Etta.

She sipped her tea and smiled across the table at him. 'This will keep you going on your drive back to Edinburgh.'

'It will,' he agreed. 'But I was wondering...' He paused and looked at her. 'Would you like to come with me? Take a wee trip to Edinburgh. Stay overnight. I'll drive you home again tomorrow or the day after that.'

Etta blinked. 'Go with you to Edinburgh this morning?'

'After we've had our breakfast. I'll book you into a nice hotel near the studio. Just a wee friendly trip to the city.'

Etta's thoughts were in a whirl. She wasn't particularly busy with her work. In fact, she planned to have a relaxing day, knitting by the fireside, and then tuning it to listen to Mullcairn's radio show in the evening. She wanted to hear what he had to say about the New Year celebrations at the castle.

'I won't be insulted if you say no,' he assured her. 'I just thought maybe you'd like to throw a few things into a wee overnight bag and come with me.'

Etta's heart was pounding, and she couldn't think of a reason why she shouldn't accept his invitation.

'Okay, I'll go with you.' She sounded delighted and excited.

Mullcairn's face lit up with a cheery smile. 'We'll have fun. Come to the studio tonight and listen to the show there. Then we'll have dinner in a nice restaurant.'

Etta started to plan what to throw into that overnight bag as they ate their breakfast.

'I'm just popping to Bradoch's bakery to buy a fresh loaf,' Muira said to Sylvia as they worked in the sweet shop. 'Do you want a scone for your morning tea?'

'Yes, whatever you're having,' said Sylvia.

Muira put her coat on. 'I won't be long.'

'Don't rush. The shop's not been busy this morning. I think everyone's sleeping off all the excitement of Hogmanay.'

Many of the shops were still closed, though the bakery, the wee grocery shop and the sweet shop had been open as usual.

Muira nodded and headed out and along to the bakery.

Bradoch finished serving two customers and then smiled at Muira. 'What can I get for you?'

'A farmhouse loaf, two fruit scones and...' Muira gestured to the celebratory cakes in the display cabinet. 'An engagement cake.'

'For Sylvia and Laurie?' Bradoch surmised.

'Yes. I don't know if they're planning to have an engagement party or anything like that,' said Muira. 'But I'm not letting Sylvia's engagement go by without a cake.'

'Fancy? Traditional? A personal theme?' Bradoch listed various types of cakes.

'Traditional. A vanilla sponge with jam and buttercream. Sylvia would like that and I'm sure Laurie will.'

They settled on a round cake with white royal icing.

'I'll pipe their names on the top,' said Bradoch.

Happy with her plan, Muira went back to the sweet shop.

Gaven put two large towels in a holdall, and looked out the window of his turret. In the distance, the loch glistened like liquid silver in the mid–morning light. The countryside was covered with snow, and he knew how cold the loch would be, but he was keen to go for a swim, as he always did on the first of January.

Wearing his running gear, he glanced at the bagpipes on the dresser. He'd put them in the protective case Laurie had given him.

Picking up his holdall, he headed down the spiral staircase.

Walter and Jessy were waiting for him in reception.

'Shall we go?' Gaven said, leading them outside to his car.

Driving down to the loch, they chatted about the previous night and what a great success the ball had been.

'Mullcairn checked out this morning,' said Walter. 'I wasn't on duty. But we'll need to tune in to his show tonight to hear what he has to say about attending the New Year ball at the castle.'

'Yes, I want to hear that,' said Gaven, driving towards the loch. They were the first to arrive. They got out of the car.

'Maybe everyone else has decided to stay in their cosy cottages,' Walter suggested.

'There's Bee!' Jessy pointed to Bee walking towards them from the other side of the loch. She was wearing a warm jacket, leggings and boots and carrying a bag containing her towel.

The air was calm but cold, and the surface of the loch looked smooth as glass.

An ice blue sky emerged through the morning haze, and sunlight glinted off the loch.

The grass and wild greenery around the edges of the loch were iced white and glistening.

Bee waved to them and trudged on through the snow.

A figure appeared in the distance behind her.

Campbell hurried to catch up with Bee. A rolled up towel was clasped in his hand, and he wore training gear, ready to strip off to his trunks for the swim.

A handful of others started to appear from various directions, some driving up, others, like Sean, had walked down from his farmhouse. His trunks were hidden by his thick cords, worn with a chunky cable knit jumper.

Robin's cottage was nearby, and she stepped out wearing her swimsuit and a towelling robe to keep her warm while she walked the short distance down to the loch. Oliver was with her. He wore his swimming trunks and had a towel draped around his shoulders. They'd gone swimming together in the turquoise sea at the nearby cove during the summer, but never in the loch.

Ian and Rose walked together to the loch from the field where their cottages were situated. They'd heard about the beautiful coast and that it was popular for swimming in the summer months, but as fairly new arrivals to the village, they'd yet to experience the delights of the shore. Now they were facing the freezing loch. Ian was up for the challenge.

Despite Rose saying she'd wave to Ian from the edge of the loch, she had a towel in a bag and looked like she was going to go in for a swim with Ian.

Fyn drove up with Aileen. She'd changed her mind too, and had closed her quilt shop to join in.

Neil pulled up in his car with Penny. They wore their swimwear and had warm clothes and towels in the back of the car. They hadn't gone swimming in the loch before.

'I've never driven a car while just wearing swimming trunks,' Neil announced as they approached the others.

'A new experience for you, Neil,' Walter said with a smile.

Penny eyed the loch and shivered. 'So is swimming in the loch in the snow.'

'Will I put the kettle on for our morning tea and scones?' Muira said to Sylvia after they'd refilled the jars in the sweet shop.

Sylvia looked at the old–fashioned clock that sat on one of the shelves. It was almost eleven.

'Are you rethinking about going for a swim?' Muira said, reading her well.

'Do you think we should go? The shop's not been busy at all. And we've packed the online orders.'

Muira reached under the counter and lifted up a bag she'd brought with her containing her swimming costume and a towel. Just in case she needed them.

Sylvia smiled.

'We could go for a paddle,' said Muira.

'Let's do it!'

They locked the shop's front door and went through to Sylvia's bedroom.

Sylvia rummaged around to find her swimming costume and put it on.

Muira hurried to change into her swimsuit. 'They'll probably have gone for a dip by now,' said Muira. 'We'd better put a spurt on.'

'I'll drive us up.' Sylvia took her engagement ring off, put it in the velvet box, grabbed a towel, stuffed it in a bag, and then they hurried out to the car.

Gaven was talking to Sean and Campbell as everyone got ready to go in for their swim. 'I don't go in the loch for long, just enough to swim around a wee bit.'

Laurie had driven down from his cabin. He didn't expect to see Sylvia, and concentrated on the loch, limbering up.

By now, all the men were standing at the side of the loch in their swimming trunks, shivering and gearing up for the icy dip.

Bee, Rose and Jessy wore their swimming costumes. Rose and Jessy had towels around their shoulders for futile warmth, preparing to throw them aside before wading in.

But Bee seemed happy to brave the cold in her swimsuit. She was tempted to dive right in, but waited until everyone was ready, especially Gaven.

'Here's Sylvia and Muira,' said Rose, seeing the car drive up.

They got out of the car, leaving their towels in the back seat.

Laurie ran over to greet Sylvia. 'I'm so pleased you decided to join in the swimming.'

'We're paddling,' Sylvia told him.

'Paddling is fine,' said Laurie.

'Okay, everyone ready?' Gaven called out to them.

Some were nodding and smiling, others looked hesitant.

Gaven stood at the edge of the loch, and taking a deep breath, he dived in.

Bee was the first to follow his lead.

Campbell dived in after Bee. He'd gone swimming in the loch one night in autumn and knew how cold it could be.

Several of them waded in, gasping and laughing, and then took the plunge and began swimming.

'Jings, it's brisk,' Sean called over to Laurie as they swam past each other.

'Oh, yes!' Laurie agreed and kept going. It was cold, refreshing, an exciting challenge and he was happy to join in the fun.

Jessy had ventured in for a paddle, and this encouraged Sylvia and Muira to do the same.

'Oh, it's freezing!' Sylvia squealed.

Laurie smiled over at her as she paddled near the edge.

Ian had encouraged Rose to wade in up to her waist. The shrieks from Rose could be heard far and wide. Ian kept laughing.

Bee was swimming at speed, relishing it. Accustomed to the cold waters further north, swimming in all weathers, she was enjoying herself.

Campbell swam under the surface at times and then emerged, shaking the water from his face.

Laurie had never gone swimming in the winter, but he swam over to Sylvia, smiling even though the loch was icy cold.

Sean sharked over to Muira and waved. 'Are you coming in for a dook?'

Muira shook her head. 'No, the water's freezing cauld.'

Rose's shrieks subsided as she became accustomed to the cold, though she didn't intend being in for long.

Gaven powered along part of the loch and then double–backed.

'I thought Etta would've been here,' Walter called over to Jessy as he swam by. She usually came down from her cottage for a paddle or with flasks of hot tea.

'Etta's away to Edinburgh with Mullcairn,' Jessy called back, initiating a few surprised looks from others. 'She phoned to say she'd be back tomorrow or the next day. Mullcairn whisked her off after breakfast.'

'Etta and Mullcairn are fair getting on well,' Muira said, hinting of a romance in the offing.

'They're just friends, at the moment,' said Jessy.

Several of the swimmers and paddlers began stepping out of the loch. They grabbed their towels, and got dried off and ready to head home.

Laurie swam over to Sylvia and then stood up and waded towards her.

Sylvia was glad that the cold helped to keep her blushes at bay, though her heart fluttered seeing the rivulets of water running over Laurie's lean–muscled body.

Laurie lifted Sylvia up and carried her out of the water. Sylvia giggled as he placed her down gently.

Sean clasped Muira's hand to steady her as she stepped from the loch.

Sylvia ran over to her car, grabbed the towels and ran back, handing one of them to Muira and wrapping the other around herself.

Gaven, Bee and Campbell were the last to step out.

There was cheerful chatter, laughter, shivering and a sense of fun amid the participants.

'Thanks again for joining me,' Gaven told them, putting on his running gear.

Laurie had now dried himself off and wore the clothes he'd driven down in. He swept his wet hair back from his face, leaned close to Sylvia and gave her a kiss. 'Are you going to the sledging tonight?'

'Yes, to watch you slide by,' Sylvia told him with a cheery smile.

Laurie smiled at her. 'Maybe you'll change your mind about that later.'

'Maybe,' said Sylvia. Then she hurried to her car with Muira, turned the heater up and drove off back to the sweet shop to get showered and dressed.

Everyone was keen to get home or back to their work after their adventure at the loch. But with another adventure scheduled that evening, the fun was far from over.

CHAPTER FIFTEEN

Laurie finished working on his songwriting and got dressed in his warm running gear to take part in the sledging.

Walking across the snow towards the castle, the windows and entrance were aglow in the night.

He saw lanterns had been lit to light up the slopes where the sledging was due to take place. Some hung from the trees, creating that fairytale atmosphere he loved.

The air felt charged with excitement, and as he got nearer to the castle, he noticed that the reception was abuzz with activity. Staff hurried in and out, preparing for the fun event.

Walter and Jessy were standing behind the front desk.

'Laurie!' Walter beckoned to him urgently as he walked into the reception.

Heading over, Laurie wondered if something was wrong.

'Mullcairn's radio show is due to start in a wee while,' said Walter. 'He's told listeners that on tonight's show he's talking about the New Year ball at the castle. Playing a special piece of music. And making an announcement. From his tone, we think he's going to tell his listeners that you're engaged to Sylvia.'

Laurie smiled, grateful for the heads up from Walter. 'Yes, I said he could tell them, but I'd love to hear Mullcairn's show tonight.'

'It clashes with the sledging,' Jessy said, sounding disappointed.

'But I'm planning to tune in on my phone,' said Walter.

'I'll do the same,' Laurie agreed.

Gaven came hurrying down the stairs dressed in dark running gear that was suitable for the sledging.

Walter told him about Mullcairn's show.

'We'll try to listen in,' said Gaven.

Walter suddenly had an idea. 'I've got an old portable radio in my shed. I'll stick new batteries in it.' He hurried away to do this.

Sylvia locked the sweet shop's front door and stood outside waiting for Sean to drive up with Muira. Wearing a warm jacket, trousers, a cosy jumper and a knitted hat and mitts, she was prepared to take part in the sledging.

She took a moment to look at the main street that was covered in snow. The shop window displays were lit up with twinkle lights, but the shops were closed for the evening. Soon, it would be time to take the Christmas tree down in the sweet shop, but she'd agreed with Muira that they'd keep the clear twinkle lights up in the window for a wee while longer.

And she thought about Laurie, excited to see him at the sledging.

Sean's car headlights lit up the snow on the main street as he pulled up with Muira. They were both warmly dressed.

Sylvia got into the back seat, and Sean drove off, heading away from the main street, by the loch and up the forest road to the castle.

Sean had the car radio tuned in to Mullcairn's show, and they listened to the start of it as they drove along.

After the opening music, Mullcairn's rich, presenter's voice sounded over the radio.

'On tonight's show I have lots to tell you about my visit to the castle for the New Year ball. But first, I want to wish you all a Happy New Year! And to celebrate, I'm going to begin with a traditional song played on the bagpipes by Gaven, the laird of the castle. This rendition was recorded at Laurie's new music studio near the castle. And more exciting news to come about Laurie...'

Walter fiddled with the knobs on his radio and tuned in just in time to hear the start of the show. Inside his shed, he listened to the opening jingles, and then ran with it back to the castle as the introduction to the bagpipes was announced.

'Gaven!' Walter yelled, causing several people standing around the laird in reception to turn and stare. 'Mullcairn is playing your bagpipe performance on the radio!' He put the old–fashioned radio down on the front desk and turned up the sound so everyone could hear it.

Laurie had cut a clear recording in the studio, suitable for playing on air, though he hadn't anticipated it would be. He'd expected it was only going to be heard on the castle's website.

Gaven had given Mullcairn a copy when he'd requested it during the previous night at the ball. Hearing himself playing the bagpipes on the radio was an experience he'd long remember.

But it was time to start the sledging, and as guests and participants from the village had arrived to take part, Gaven hurried outside to the lantern–lit slopes. One slope was suitable for beginners, not too steep, a fun wee ride. The second slope offered a bit more of a challenge.

Walter followed Gaven, and carried the radio outside. Other staff were on hand to help guests if required.

'Enjoy your sledging,' Gaven announced to those gathered on the snowy slopes. 'Tea and hot chocolate will be available at the castle when you go back in.'

A selection of sledges were lined up for people to pick from. But Walter had kept the old–fashioned sledges he'd repaired aside for Laurie, Ian, Sean, Campbell and others to use.

Laurie had followed Gaven and picked one of Walter's sledges.

Sylvia had arrived with Muira and Sean. She trudged across the snow, waving to Laurie.

'There's room for two on this sledge,' Laurie said, encouraging her to sit in the front.

Sylvia sat down and tugged her hat on tight. 'Don't go too fast.'

'Hold on tight!' Laurie pushed off from the back of the sledge, taking the steeper slope, but keeping the speed reasonable.

Sylvia's gleeful squeals sounded all the way down, and at the bottom she was eager for them to have another go.

Laurie pulled the sledge back up the slope, using the side route as others slid down on their sledges. At the top again, Sylvia sat in front, but this time she'd changed her mind about the speed. 'Faster this time,' she said, smiling.

Pushing off with extra power, Laurie jumped in.

'Wheee!' Sylvia said, enjoying the fun.

Walter had sat the radio down in the snow where he could listen to it while attending to the sledging. Gaven stood beside him, listening too.

'*I wore my kilt and sporran to the ball and joined in the ceilidh dances at the castle, and the ballroom dances,*' Mullcairn told his listeners, adding details about the music and the delicious buffet.

Appreciating Mullcairn doing this and giving the castle a mention, Gaven phoned the radio studio to leave a thank you message for the presenter.

'You're through to the Mullcairn show,' an assistant said. The show encouraged listeners to call and often included phone–in chats. 'Can I have your name and where you're calling from?'

'I'm Gaven, the laird of the castle that Mullcairn was kind enough to mention on the show. I just wanted to thank him—'

The assistant's interest was immediate. 'Oh, you're the laird! Hold on while I put you through to Mullcairn. I'm sure he'll want to include you in a live chat.'

'No! I only wanted to thank him,' Gaven cut–in.

Ignoring his objections, he was put through to Mullcairn.

'Gaven, don't worry, you're not live on air yet. The jingles are playing,' Mullcairn assured him.

'I only phoned to thank you,' Gaven tried to explain.

'You're welcome, but while you're on the line, I'll get you to say a few words to the listeners.'

'What do you want me to say?' said Gaven.

'Wish them a Happy New Year, and then we'll chat for a moment.' Mullcairn made it sound easy.

Before Gaven could consider this, the jingles finished and Mullcairn introduced him.

'*I've got Gaven live on the line tonight. Here's a wee message from the laird of the castle himself.*'

Gaven took a deep breath. '*I'd like to wish your listeners a Happy New Year.*'

'*That was some fine bagpipe playing we heard from you. And I had the pleasure of seeing you play live on Hogmanay outside the castle in the snow.*'

'*Thank you. I was accompanied by Laurie playing the bagpipes outside. We'd rehearsed a few times at his new recording studio, then played live on the night of the ball to ring in the New Year.*'

'*I had a magnificent time dancing at the ball. I danced with Etta. She's here tonight at the studio. I'm giving her a wee wave through the window as she has a cup of tea while listening to the show.*'

Etta perked up, nearly spilling her tea. She was sitting in the guest area just outside the studio and could see Mullcairn doing his live show. They were having dinner later and he'd invited her along to the studio. She hadn't expected him to mention her. Staring through at him, she looked unsure what to do.

'*Oh, she's waving and giving me a cheery smile*,' Mullcairn lied. Then he continued to chat to Gaven, but he could hear happy chaos in the background. '*What's going on at the castle tonight? Another party by the sounds of it.*'

'*I'm outside the castle in the snow. Guests are enjoying an evening of sledging.*'

'*Och! I'd love to have joined in*,' said Mullcairn.

'*We're having other nights and afternoons of sledging, so if you're here, join in with us*,' Gaven offered.

'*I will.*' Mullcairn glanced at Etta, giving her a nod that he intended doing this. Then he got ready to reveal the latest news.

Gaven was still on the line.

'*I promised I had exciting news about Laurie*,' Mullcairn told the listeners. '*After playing the bagpipes with Gaven outside the castle, Laurie got down on one kilted knee and proposed to his lovely girlfriend, Sylvia, the wonderful classical pianist I've mentioned to you before on the show. And she said, yes. He'd kept the engagement ring in his sporran all evening.*'

Walter grinned at Gaven as they stood at the top of the slope listening to the show on the radio as guests slid down on the sledges.

'*I had the privilege of seeing a wee clip of Laurie proposing to Sylvia.*' Mullcairn spoke directly to Gaven. '*When will the video of the New Year ball be on the castle's website?*'

'*I put it up on the website before I came outside for the sledging,*' Gaven told Mullcairn. '*And there are clips of you ceilidh dancing in your kilt and doing the samba with Etta.*'

'*Do you here that, folks? If you want to see me giving it laldy on the dance floor, check out the video on the castle's website. Most of you know what I look like, but it'll let others put a face, kilt and sporran to the voice you hear on the radio. And remember to take a peek at Laurie's proposal.*'

Nearby, Laurie and Sylvia had stopped to listen to Mullcairn's announcement on Laurie's phone.

Sylvia smiled excitedly at Laurie.

Others were tuning in on their phones including Sean and Muira standing at the side of the slopes.

'*I wish Laurie and Sylvia all the best,*' Mullcairn said cheerily. '*I don't know if they're having an engagement party or if they have a date for their wedding. But if I hear any more news about this, I'll let you know on the show.*'

Laurie looked at Sylvia, wondering if she wanted an engagement party, and if they should be thinking of a wedding date. 'I hadn't thought about an engagement party,' he said.

Sylvia smiled brightly. 'It would be nice, but we don't have to.'

'I want you to come and see the house, hopefully tomorrow night, if you're not busy. I would've invited you this evening but...' He gestured around at the sledging.

'There's barely been any time to spare. I'm still in a whirlwind from the ball and the proposal,' Sylvia admitted.

'I feel the same. So how about I organise a party at the house tomorrow evening around seven? We'll invite Muira, Sean and others.'

Sylvia nodded. 'Yes, that would be great. A wee get together, and everyone will see your new house and the studio. It'll be like a housewarming and engagement party.'

'But I'd like you to be there early, around six–thirty,' said Laurie. 'I want you to see the house first, when it's just the two of us.'

'Okay.' Sylvia smiled, feeling excited.

'And there's something special I want to show you,' Laurie added.

'What is it?'

'It's a surprise.'

Sylvia smiled. 'I love surprises.'

'*Well, I'll let you get on with your sledging night, Gaven,*' said Mullcairn. '*Thanks for calling and chatting on the show.*'

And Gaven's phone was switched back to the assistant as Mullcairn continued on air.

Ian and Rose slid by on a sledge, enjoying themselves, as did others including Fyn and Aileen.

Laurie put his phone in his pocket and joined in the sledging fun with Sylvia. And they told Muira, Sean and others about the party, inviting them to come along.

Bradoch had turned up for the sledging, and Laurie took the chance to order cakes and pastries for the party, and arranged to pick them up from the bakery in the afternoon.

Later, Bradoch whispered to Muira. 'I'll have the engagement cake ready for tomorrow night and bring it with me.'

'Thanks, Bradoch,' said Muira.

As the evening wore on, flakes of snow began to flutter down, and Gaven invited guests to go inside for a warming cup of hot chocolate.

Laurie kissed Sylvia goodnight outside the castle as the evening ended and everyone started to head home.

Sean and Muira were waiting for her in the car.

'I'll see you tomorrow night, and I'll be there early,' Sylvia promised him.

Laurie smiled as she hurried away and got into Sean's car. He waved them off and then walked back to his cabin.

The snow was falling heavier now. Laurie looked around at the winter scenery, the trees covered in snow against the dark sky. Soon, he'd be leaving the cabin and living in his own house. But he wanted Sylvia to see the house first.

Laurie's day sparked in as he got everything ready for the party. In the afternoon, he'd picked up the order from Bradoch's bakery and set up the food and drinks in his new kitchen.

He'd unpacked the housewarming gifts and put them in the kitchen and the living room. The beautiful music theme quilt that the crafting bee ladies had made for him looked lovely folded over the back of the couch. Rose's appliqué cushion covers added a stylish touch. And he liked the assortment of gifts for the kitchen, from the oven mitts and tea cosies to the tea towels and egg cosies.

The music studio was set to let everyone have a look around. Laurie looked at the piano, hoping that Sylvia would like her surprise gift.

News of his engagement had hit the headlines, and he'd had to deal with messages from his manager that the media wanted to confirm this was true and glean a few quotes from him. Laurie knew that appearing in news articles was part of his lifestyle and handled the press enquires well via his manager.

Checking the time, he got dressed in a classy pair of dark trousers and put on a sky blue shirt.

Sylvia was due to arrive, and there she was, driving up to the house.

Laurie opened the front door to welcome her. The daylight had already given way to the early evening.

Wearing dark blue velvet trousers tucked into her boots, and a white jumper under her warm coat, Sylvia stepped out of the car into the snow. She'd brought a bag filled with chocolates and other sweets.

Laurie hurried over to greet her, lifting her off her feet in a huge, welcoming hug.

When he put her down, Sylvia looked around at the snow–covered fields that surrounded the property. Everything glistened in the evening glow. She breathed in the crisp, fresh air. 'What a beautiful night.'

'Come on,' he said, clasping her hand. 'I'll show you the house, and then the studio.'

Eager for the tour, Sylvia walked with him and stepped inside the house.

Laurie hung her coat up and she put her bag down in the hall, then walked through to the living room.

'This is gorgeous,' she said, admiring the light, neutral colour scheme and the watercolour paintings on the walls. She smiled when she saw the quilt.

He gave her a whirlwind tour of the rest of the house, wanting to make sure he had time to show her the studio before everyone arrived.

'Come and see the studio,' he beckoned to her. A door led through from the house to the studio, but he wanted her to enter from the front door, so they stepped outside and walked the short distance to the side of the house.

They stepped into the small hallway where he'd hung his bagpipes back up on the wall.

He led her through to the studio.

The first things she noticed were the guitars, keyboard, and all the recording deck equipment. Then she turned around.

'Oh, my goodness,' she said. 'You've got a baby grand piano!'

Laurie smiled at her.

Sylvia went over to admire the classic black piano.

'Sit down and try it,' he said.

Sylvia sat down. 'This is like the one in the piano bar, the type I used to love playing years ago.'

He'd remembered her telling him this. It was part of the reason he'd chosen it.

She began playing one of her favourite classical songs. 'It sounds wonderful here in the studio. The tone is so rich and vibrant.'

'I'm glad you approve.'

Her playing filled the studio with the beautiful sound of the piano.

'You do know that I'll be coming here to play your piano,' she told him lightly.

'*Your* piano, Sylvia.'

She stopped playing and glanced round at him.

The look he gave her confirmed that he'd bought it for her.

'Surprise,' he said.

Sylvia stood up and threw her arms around Laurie, hugging the breath from him. 'This is too much, but I love it. And I love you.'

Seeing her reaction touched his heart. The planning for the proposal and the piano had finally worked out well. 'I love you too.' He kissed her and hugged her tight.

She ran over to the piano and started playing again, another classical piece, but a light lit up on the studio wall, a silent indication that someone was at the front door of the house.

Hurrying outside with Laurie, Sylvia saw Muira and Sean standing at the front door. Car headlights illuminated the narrow road as the other guests arrived.

Sylvia couldn't contain her joy. 'Laurie has bought me a beautiful baby grand piano! It's in the music studio. I've just been playing it and the tone is wonderful!' She tugged at Muira and Sean. 'You have to come and see it.'

Swept up in Sylvia's enthusiasm, they hurried away with her to view the piano while Laurie welcomed the guests into the house as they arrived, telling them about his surprise gift for her.

Bradoch carried a white cake box into the kitchen. 'This is from Muira.' He glanced around. 'Is she here yet?'

'Yes, I'm here,' Muira said, hurrying in with Sean and Sylvia to join the party. 'Sylvia was showing me her new piano.'

'You'll all see it later,' said Sylvia, wanting to enjoy the party in the house.

Gaven turned up with Walter and Jessy. Rose was there with Ian. Everyone had arrived and the party started with Muira presenting the happy couple with the engagement cake.

Bradoch had iced their names on top of the cake, and after Sylvia and Laurie were photographed with it, he expertly cut it into pieces that were shared with all the guests. Etta was still in Edinburgh with Mullcairn and not due back until the following day, but two pieces of cake were kept for them.

A celebratory toast filled the kitchen with cheers and smiles, and then Laurie gave the guests a tour of the house, followed by tucking into the buffet. From cakes and scones to sandwiches and savoury pastries, they all enjoyed the food.

'We can go through this way to the studio,' Laurie told them after they'd had something to eat and drink.

'I've never seen inside a music studio,' said Jessy.

'Neither have I,' Rose added.

Spotlights illuminated the studio as everyone walked in, fascinated to have a look around.

'It's an impressive studio,' Bradoch said to Laurie.

Neil and Fyn were interested in seeing the technical equipment, as was Oliver.

'It's so quiet, except for our chatter,' Aileen remarked.

'The studio is sound proofed,' Laurie told her.

'It must be nice to sort of switch off from the world and be in your own calm bubble,' said Bradoch. 'That's what I like about working in the bakery early in the morning before most folk are up.'

'It is,' Laurie agreed.

'Is this where you were rehearsing the bagpipes?' Walter said to Gaven.

'Yes, and Laurie encouraged me to play that red guitar.' Gaven gestured to the electric guitar on a stand beside the other guitars and instruments.

'I didn't know you could play the guitar, Gaven.' Fyn sounded impressed.

'I can't play it properly,' said Gaven. 'I was just fooling around with it. I'd always wanted to feel what it was like to play an electric guitar.'

'Gaven can read music,' Laurie chimed–in. 'And he plays the bagpipes well. I know it's a different instrument, but he has the musicality in him.'

'Are you going to play your new piano?' Muira said to Sylvia.

'Maybe I can encourage her to play something we can dance to,' said Laurie. 'There's no dance floor in the studio, but I'm sure we can make do and get the party going before we go back through to the house.'

'I'll play the piano if you accompany me on your guitar, and sing,' Sylvia said, smiling as she bargained with him.

Laurie picked up the red electric guitar, plugged it in, but instead of starting to play it, he handed the guitar to Gaven. 'Here you go. Let's celebrate with our own wee band.'

Gaven smiled as he accepted the guitar.

'Have you got a triangle I can ting?' Walter joked.

Laurie laughed, and handed Walter a set of drumsticks. 'I'm sure you can hit a few beats on the drums.'

Walter sat down at the drum kit. 'Oh, this is going to be wild.'

'Anyone else got a hidden talent for playing or is up to the task for fun?' said Laurie.

Neil cleared his throat. 'I used to have an acoustic guitar when I was a boy.'

Penny looked astonished. She was still finding things out about her new husband. 'I didn't know you had a talent for playing the guitar.'

Neil shook his head. 'I don't. That's why I'm a goldsmith, but I can probably remember how to strum a bit.'

'Help yourself to one of the acoustic guitars,' Laurie said to Neil. 'They've all been played on my tours.'

Neil lifted one of the guitars that was the closest to the one he'd had from years ago. He trailed his fingers across the strings and nodded. 'Okay, I'm up for it.'

'I need backing singers,' Laurie announced. 'What about you, Muira, and you Jessy?'

Muira and Jessy encouraged Bee, Aileen and Rose to participate.

Laurie then plugged in another electric guitar. 'Come on, everyone join the band and let's play!'

Laurie put his guitar strap around his neck and played the opening riff to one of his popular songs. He nodded to Sylvia, and she started to play, knowing the song well.

The sound of Laurie's guitar and the piano filled the studio, and then Laurie started to sing.

Gaven and Neil played the guitars as best they could. Walter kept a beat on the drums.

When it came to the chorus, the makeshift backing singers sung their hearts out, and were soon joined by all the others.

It wasn't the best band, but it was the most enthusiastic and fun, with all of them joining in, one way or another, all friends together.

Sylvia smiled at Laurie as she played, and he smiled back at her, sensing that they'd build a happy life together with their music and their love for each other in this wonderful village in the heart of the Scottish Highlands.

After playing in the studio, everyone went back through to the house to continue dancing and enjoy the buffet.

It was midnight when the guests started to head home after having a great time.

Laurie stood at the front door of the house with Sylvia, waving them off as they all drove away.

He wrapped his arms around Sylvia, shielding her from the cold night air.

Sylvia gazed up at the stars in the sky as snowflakes started to fall gently. She was the last to leave. Another busy day at the sweet shop beckoned, but so did an exciting future with Laurie.

Laurie held her close as they kissed goodnight.

'I love you,' she said.

'I love you too, Sylvia,' he murmured, and then kissed her again.

Sylvia gazed up at him and smiled as the snow fell like starlight, looking forward to their happy life together.

Laurie waved Sylvia off and then went into his studio, feeling the ending lyrics for one of his songs begin to filter through his mind. Picking up his guitar he started to play and sing...

Music and dance
My heart is in tune with you
Rhythm and romance
I promise my love is true
We'll make a home together
My house is yours forever
A Happy New Year and a home for two.

End

About the Author:

De-ann Black is a bestselling author, scriptwriter and former newspaper journalist. She has over 100 books published. Romance, thrillers, espionage novels, action adventure. And children's books (non-fiction rocket science books and children's fiction). She became an Amazon All-Star author in 2014 and 2015.

She previously worked as a full-time newspaper journalist for several years. She had her own weekly columns in the press. This included being a motoring correspondent where she got to test drive cars every week for the press for three years.

Before being asked to work for the press, De-ann worked in magazine editorial writing everything from fashion features to social news. She was the marketing editor of a glossy magazine.

She is also a professional artist and illustrator. Embroidery design, fabric design, dressmaking, sewing, knitting and fashion are part of her work.

Additionally, De-ann has always been interested in fitness, and was a fitness and bodybuilding champion, 100 metre runner and mountaineer. As a former N.A.B.B.A. Miss Scotland, she had a weekly fitness show on the radio that ran for over three years.

De-ann trained in Shukokai karate, boxing, kickboxing, Dayan Qigong and Jiu Jitsu. She is currently based in Scotland.

Her 16 colouring books are available in paperback, including her latest Summer Nature Colouring Book and Flower Nature Colouring Book.

Her latest embroidery pattern books include: Floral Garden Embroidery Patterns, Christmas & Winter Embroidery Patterns, Floral Spring Embroidery Patterns and Sea Theme Embroidery Patterns.

Website: Find out more at: www.de-annblack.com

Fabric, Wallpaper & Home Decor Collections:
De-ann's fabric designs and wallpaper collections, and home decor items, including her popular Scottish Garden Thistles patterns, are available from Spoonflower.
www.de-annblack.com/spoonflower

Also by De-ann Black (Romance, Action/Thrillers & Children's books). See her Amazon Author page or website for further details about her books, screenplays, illustrations, art, fabric designs and embroidery patterns.

Amazon Author page:
www.De-annBlack.com/Amazon

Romance books:

Scottish Loch Romance series:
1. Sewing & Mending Cottage
2. Scottish Loch Summer Romance
3. Sweet Music
4. Knitting Bee
5. Autumn Romance
6. Christmas Ballroom Dancing
7. Scottish Highlands New Year Ball

Music, Dance & Romance series:
1. The Sweetest Waltz
2. Knitting & Starlight
3. Ballroom Dancing Christmas Romance

Snow Bells Haven series:
1. Snow Bells Christmas
2. Snow Bells Wedding
3. Love & Lyrics

Scottish Highlands & Island Romance series:
1. Scottish Island Knitting Bee
2. Scottish Island Fairytale Castle
3. Vintage Dress Shop on the Island
4. Fairytale Christmas on the Island

Sewing, Crafts & Quilting series:
1. The Sewing Bee
2. The Sewing Shop
3. Knitting Cottage (Scottish Highland romance)
4. Scottish Highlands Christmas Wedding

Quilting Bee & Tea Shop series:
1. The Quilting Bee
2. The Tea Shop by the Sea
3. Embroidery Cottage
4. Knitting Shop by the Sea
5. Christmas Weddings

The Cure for Love Romance series:
1. The Cure for Love
2. The Cure for Love at Christmas

Cottages, Cakes & Crafts series:
1. The Flower Hunter's Cottage
2. The Sewing Bee by the Sea
3. The Beemaster's Cottage
4. The Chocolatier's Cottage
5. The Bookshop by the Seaside
6. The Dressmaker's Cottage

Scottish Chateau, Colouring & Crafts series:
1. Christmas Cake Chateau
2. Colouring Book Cottage

Summer Sewing Bee
Heather Park: Regency Romance

Sewing, Knitting & Baking series:
1. The Tea Shop
2. The Sewing Bee & Afternoon Tea
3. The Christmas Knitting Bee
4. Champagne Chic Lemonade Money
5. The Vintage Sewing & Knitting Bee

Tea Dress Shop series:
1. The Tea Dress Shop At Christmas
2. The Fairytale Tea Dress Shop In Edinburgh
3. The Vintage Tea Dress Shop In Summer

The Tea Shop & Tearoom series:
1. The Christmas Tea Shop & Bakery
2. The Christmas Chocolatier
3. The Chocolate Cake Shop in New York at Christmas
4. The Bakery by the Seaside
5. Shed in the City

Christmas Romance series:
1. Christmas Romance in Paris
2. Christmas Romance in Scotland

Oops! I'm the Paparazzi series:
1. Oops! I'm the Paparazzi
2. Oops! I'm Up To Mischief
3. Oops! I'm the Paparazzi, Again

The Bitch-Proof Suit series:
1. The Bitch-Proof Suit
2. The Bitch-Proof Romance
3. The Bitch-Proof Bride
4. The Bitch-Proof Wedding

Dublin Girl
Why Are All The Good Guys Total Monsters?
I'm Holding Out For A Vampire Boyfriend

Action/Thriller books:

Knight in Miami
Agency Agenda
Love Him Forever
Someone Worse

Electric Shadows
The Strife Of Riley
Shadows Of Murder
Cast a Dark Shadow

Children's books:

Faeriefied
Secondhand Spooks
Poison-Wynd

Wormhole Wynd
Science Fashion
School For Aliens

Colouring books:

Summer Nature
Flower Nature
Summer Garden
Spring Garden
Autumn Garden
Sea Dream
Festive Christmas
Christmas Garden
Christmas Theme

Flower Bee
Wild Garden
Faerie Garden Spring
Flower Hunter
Stargazer Space
Bee Garden
Scottish Garden
Seasons

Embroidery Design books:

Sea Theme Embroidery Patterns
Floral Garden Embroidery Patterns
Christmas & Winter Embroidery Patterns
Floral Spring Embroidery Patterns
Floral Nature Embroidery Designs
Scottish Garden Embroidery Designs

Printed in Great Britain
by Amazon

54887913R00126